HOLY PLACES OF CELTIC BRITAIN

HOLY PLACES
of
CELTIC BRITAIN

A Photographic Portrait of
Sacred Albion

WRITTEN AND PHOTOGRAPHED BY
MICK SHARP

BLANDFORD

To Julie, a sister worth waiting for

A BLANDFORD BOOK

First published in the UK 1997 by Blandford
A Cassell Imprint
Cassell Plc, Wellington House,
125 Strand, London WC2R 0BB

Distributed in the United States by Sterling Publishing Co.,
Inc., 387 Park Avenue South, New York, NY 10016-8810

**A Cataloguing-in-Publication Data entry for this title is
available from the British Library**

ISBN 0-7137-2642-3

Printed and bound by Dah Hua Printing Press Co., Hong Kong

CONTENTS

ACKNOWLEDGEMENTS

ANY PEOPLE have contributed to this book, although it will come as a surprise to some of them. The main written sources used are given in the Bibliography, with directly quoted extracts and opinions credited in the text.

I am particularly beholden to Gerald Wait who generously gave me a copy of his PhD thesis, 'Ritual and Religion in the Iron Age of Britain'. Packed with detail and analysis, it is a major source for Celtic religious beliefs and practices.

Other useful information concerning specific sites, and the Celts in general, was supplied by Simant Bostock (Glastonbury); Kathryn and Peter Conway, and Leonna Forrest (Glen Lyon); David Dunkin and John Funnell (Sussex); Kate Geary, Dave Longley and Dave Thompson of the Gwynedd Archaeological Trust; Matt at Flag Fen; Jo May, owner of Boleigh Fogou; Susan Seright of Groam House Museum, Rosemarkie; and Diane Williams of Cadw.

The staff of the reference library in Dumfries and the Centre for Oxfordshire Studies were especially efficient and helpful.

I am grateful to the following for facilitating or kindly granting permission for photography: Steve Benfield of the Colchester Archaeological Trust at Gosbecks Archaeological Park; Jane Bircher, Keeper of Collections, and the friendly staff at the Roman Baths Museum at Bath; Neil Bray of English Heritage at Lullingstone Roman villa; Evelyn Davies at Pennant Melangell; Mick Markie for taking me to Isle Maree; Mike Olney at Flag Fen Archaeology Park; Peter Proudlove of Kingfisher Cruises, who took me to Eileach an Naoimh; and Paquita Webb, who organized an enjoyable morning in Wookey Hole Caves.

With tact and persistence, Maggy Mason and Dave Thompson managed to lodge a few basic rules of English usage in my thick head.

Accommodation, general help and encouragement along the way were provided by Phil Abramson; Claire Adamson; Brian and Lynn Ayers; Hubert and Monica Beales; Richard Bryant; Donna and Phil Cunningham; Graham and Julie Hayman; Carolyn Heighway; Pat Lynch; Frank and Louise Moran; David Murphy; Charlotte Roberts; Walter Sharp; Roger and Tania Simpson; Tricia Snell; Kirstie Thornber; Brian Williamson; and Kathleen Williamson.

As ever, my greatest debt is to Jean Williamson for being entangled in most stages of this book, and dealing with many other things to enable me to finish it. Jean also provided the map, drawings, photograph of Norfolk Lavender, and was brave enough to leave me alone with her Apple Mac.

Linda Jeavons and Janet Smithies kept things running smoothly while we were gadding around Britain.

I am grateful to my editor Stuart Booth for suggesting a book on the Celts, and for seeing it through.

Despite excellent help and advice, the idiosyncrasies and mistakes – wilful and otherwise – are entirely my own.

PREFACE

I HAVE CHOSEN examples of *loca sacra* – places set apart for sacred use – to illustrate a range of Celtic religious beliefs and practices from the Late Bronze Age through to the present day. Of central importance in the spiritual life of the Celts was the natural world, certain elements of which they saw as manifestations of the longed-for otherworld. Their sensitivity and strong response to unseen forces led to the recognition and creation of holy places, the locations of which have proved more constant than their beliefs and forms of worship.

Modern views of the Celts diverge widely. At one extreme they are seen as an intercontinental phenomenon (discovering North America, etc.) coming in all shapes and sizes, held together by a cultural package and related forms of an ancestral Celtic language. The opposed view, based on Julius Caesar's description of Celts occupying one of the three divisions of Gaul, restricts them to what is now central and southern France, northern Italy and south-western Germany. This view, held by John Collis and others, maintains there were no pan-European Celtic people, no 'broad-based Celtic art, society or religion' and no Celts in Britain. Classical writers did not call the people of Britain Celts; up to the 1600s the terms 'ancient Britons' and 'British language' were used. The term 'Celtic' was imported from the Continent to denote a group of languages, before growing into the romantic, ill-defined and widely misused modern label. I have chosen a reasonably liberal interpretation of the term, and will try to chart a middle way through the Celtic minefield.

Britain first emerges from the anonymity of prehistory through the writings of Greek and Roman authors. A Greek report of a voyage taken before 530 BC, along the Spanish coast and round to the Atlantic, describes trade between the people of Brittany and the inhabitants of two large islands to the north named Ierne (Ireland) and Albion (Britain). In the late third century BC Pytheas referred to Britain and Ireland together – the modern British Isles – as the Pretanic Islands. The Romans applied the names Britannia and Britanni to Britain and her people, at the same time referring to the country north of Stirling as Caledonia.

The 'Celts' were also brought into the glare of history by classical writers applying the term, rather imprecisely, to their 'barbarian' neighbours. The Greek Keltoi and Roman Celtae were versions of the name of the overall group to which many of the individual tribes, such as the Galli (Gauls), considered themselves to belong. For his own political reasons, Caesar exaggerated the differences between the Gauls and the Germani, their immediate neighbours beyond the Rhine. Although many claimed descent from the heroes of Troy, the Celts were never one race or nation but a loose and quarrelsome collection of tribes – themselves made up of extended families – ruled by kings, priests and lawgivers. Descriptions range from small and dark, through to the Celtic 'ideal' of tall, blue-eyed and very fair; they were usually impressively taller than the Romans. Tacitus, writing in the first century AD, suggests a Spanish origin for the Silures of south Wales, who had swarthy faces and curly hair. The Caledonians he links with the Germans, because of their large limbs and reddish hair, while the people on the south coast resembled the Gauls. Their excitable natures, restlessness and constantly shifting loyalties prevented a wide and stable political unity, ultimately making them vulnerable to the military organization and determined expansion of the Roman Empire.

Archaeologists have defined a material culture, evolved in Europe from Bronze Age and earlier roots, with a language group, social structure, religious beliefs and art styles which, although not uniform, are recognizably 'Celtic'. The initial unifying package from c. 800 BC onwards is named Hallstatt, after the village and cemetery in Austria where excavations in the 1840s revealed rich burials of a warrior-élite equipped with horse-riding harnesses and iron swords. Typical Hallstatt burials in central Europe were inhumations accompanied by horse-trappings and spoked four-wheeled wagons placed inside wooden chambers beneath earthen mounds. In the second major phase of Celtic culture (as defined by archaeologists), lasting from the fifth century BC until Roman times, the centres of power are believed to have shifted to the Rhineland and the Marne. Light two-wheeled chariots were used for battle, display and burial. The first large organized Celtic settlements – hillforts, proto-towns or oppida – also appear during this La Tène phase. The name comes from 'The Shallows' on the Swiss lake of Neuchâtel, where hundreds of votive offerings of metalwork, decorated with distinctive, stylized and geometric motifs, were recovered from the water in the late 1850s and 1860s. The swirling, distorted forms and disturbing beauty of La Tène art reappear later to inspire the crosses, illuminated manuscripts and decorations of the Celtic Church. Increasing wealth and trade in the first millennium BC, associated with iron-working and salt-mining, caused dramatic changes in central and western Europe. Contact with such peoples as the Greeks, who introduced them to wine, the Scythians, who demonstrated the related skills of horse-riding and wearing trousers, and the Etruscans, with their highly developed art forms, trading systems and cities, greatly influenced the Celts. The use of horses and wagons brought the traditional steppes lifestyle of nomadic pastoralism mixed with intermittent agriculture to an increasingly civilized Mediterranean world based on settled city-states. By the fourth century BC the material accompaniments of these highly mobile barbarians were to be found from the Balkans and northern Italy to Belgium, and from the Black Sea in the east to Britain in the west. Around 390 BC Rome was sacked by Celts, and another group entered Greece c. 272 BC, plundering the sacred site and oracle of Delphi. Some continued eastwards to found a colony in Asia Minor, becoming the 'foolish' Galatians chastised by St Paul in his epistle.

Their forceful but uncoordinated expansion could not be sustained. Despite set-backs, Roman power was growing, and by 250 BC it was they who possessed the Italian peninsula and, after the capture of Carthage in 146 BC, went on to control the Mediterranean. The 'barbarian' tribes of Europe were mainly subdued, brought within an empire which, at its peak in the second century AD, held sway over the lands bordering the Black Sea and Mediterranean, including Iberia and Gaul, along with the lonely Atlantic outpost of Britain. The very north of Britain, beyond the Forth and Clyde, was never properly conquered. Ireland was considered to have completely escaped the Roman yoke, although the recent discovery of a heavily defended coastal fort at Drumanagh, north of Dublin, suggests that the Romans did set foot on Irish turf. The defended beach-head, which developed into a large trading town, may have been built to support military campaigns or as part of a system for controlling Irish raids from the east coast.

In the first century AD the people of Britain were divided into over thirty main tribal groupings distributed throughout the whole country. Except for some in the far north of very ancient lineage, the tribal names are generally considered to be Celtic in form: the Iceni of East Anglia, the Brigantes of northern England and the Ordovices of central and north-west Wales are among the most familiar. The Celtic-speaking populations of Britain were once considered to have been formed by invasions of aristocratic warriors swamping the native inhabitants. Only two major continental intrusions are now generally recognized: the Arras culture in south-east Yorkshire, with cart burials that are so similar to La Tène burials in the Champagne region of France, and the Belgae, who moved from northern Gaul into south-east England. As in the rest of Europe, the British 'Celts' evolved from the indigenous Bronze Age peoples who, under the influence of trade, social contact and some settlement from the Continent, formed their own versions of the Hallstatt and La Tène 'cultures'. It was not all one-way traffic: Caesar states that the druidic system of teaching was introduced into Gaul from Britain, and highly praised items such as hunting dogs and brightly coloured woollen cloaks were exported.

After the Claudian invasion of AD 43, the Romans gradually advanced from their south-eastern power base into Wales, and to the edge of the Scottish Highlands, bringing most of the country under imperial control or influence. Many native Britons enthusiastically adopted the more appealing ways of Roman life and worship, while foreign soldiers, oppressed by the power of an alien landscape, thought it wise to appease the native gods. Ancient ways continued in many guises and those disaffected Britons still hankering after more heroic times eased their frustrations and shame through intrigue, rebellion and slaughter. By the fifth century AD the empire itself was in serious trouble, weakened by over-expansion, internal dissent and hostile barbarians from the east. In AD 410 Emperor Honorius withdrew the legions, leaving the Romano-British to defend themselves against the incursions of Angles, Saxons, Jutes and Frisians. By 450 these raiders and mercenaries from Denmark, Germany and Holland were settling and farming.

A colony of Britons had formed in Brittany by 460, while others withdrew to the west of Britain, especially Cornwall, Cumbria and Wales, where a version of 'Roman' life continued. Those who stayed put in the east gradually merged with the newcomers to varying degrees. The Anglo-Saxon westward advance was resisted under the leadership of several resourceful Romano-British chieftains, such as Ambrosius Aurelianus, whose brave exploits and characteristics were amalgamated into the legendary figure of King Arthur. By the ninth century the Anglo-Saxons and Romano-British in the four great kingdoms of Wessex, Mercia, East Anglia and Northumberland had formed the basis of an 'English' society, to be further shaped and changed by Vikings, Scandinavians and Normans. Within this proto-England, 'British' communities remained and much English folklore and custom, especially in such areas as northern Derbyshire, continued 'Celtic' traditions.

The main concern of this book is to look at some of the evidence of religious expression and ritual behaviour connected with places and landscapes in what has come to be regarded as 'Celtic Britain'. Those areas which have most obviously retained, revived or reinvented their Celtic roots will feature most strongly in the chapters on Celtic Christianity and continuity. For the pre-Roman Iron Age and Romano-Celtic periods, examples from many parts of Britain will be used, along with references to archaeological and written material from Ireland and the Continent to give a fuller picture of Celtic customs.

Mick Sharp, Gwynedd

MAP OF SITES

St Ninian's Isle

Shetland Isles

0   50   100 miles
0 50 100 150 km

Isle Maree
Munlochy
Burghead
Craigie Well
St Mary's Well, Culloden
Well of the Heads
St Finnan's Isle
Schiehallion
Tigh nam Bodach
St Fillan's Pool
Iona
Dunino Den
Eileach an Naoimh
Clackmannan
Dunadd
Bar Hill
St Columba's Cave
Cairnpapple Hill
St Blane's
Holy Island (Lindisfarne)
Holy Island, Arran
Eildon Hill
Newstead
Dowloch
Lady's Well
Coventina's Well
Benwell
St Columba's Footsteps
Castle Loch
Temple of Mithras
Wren's Egg
Clochmaben
St Ninian's Cave
Maryport
Derwentwater
Newtondale Spring
Druid's Temple
Ingleborough
Wetwang
Swastika Stone
Puffin Island and Penmon Priory
Julian's Bower
Llaneilian
Lindow Common
St Anne's Well
Sherwood Forest
St Gwenfaen's Well
Holywell
River Witham
Llyn Cerrig Bach
Chester
Alderley Edge
Pistyll
Dinas Emrys
Norfolk Lavender
St Mary's Well (Ffynnon Fair)
Overton
Tissington
Bardsey Island
Pennant Melangell
Wing
Flag Fen
Burgh Castle
Croft Ambrey
Bartlow Hills
Castell Henllys
Ippollits
Carn Ingli
Partrishow
Charlton-on-Otmoor
Gosbecks
Ffynnon Gwenlais
Virtuous Well
Woodeaton
Harlow
St David's
Caerwent
Runnymede
Bradwell-on-Sea
St Non's Well
Tarren Deusant
Uffington
Syon Reach
Caldey Island
Steep Holme
Nettleton Shrub
Lullingstone
Burry Holms
Llantwit Major
Bath
Casterley Camp
Brean Down
Wilsford
Farley Heath
Chittlehampton
Wookey
Danebury Ring
Glastonbury
Mizmaze
Chanctonbury Ring
Cadbury Castle
Cerne Abbas
St Nectan's Kieve
St Clether
Maiden Castle
Hayling Island
St Non's Well, Altarnun
Wistman's Wood
Jordan Hill
Meavy
Madron
Roche
Sancreed
St Melor's Well
Boleigh

CHAPTER ONE

THE
PAGAN
CELTS

N ANIMISM gods as such do not exist, but an elemental force in all objects can be dominated by a shaman-magician. The religion of the pre-Roman Celts seems to have been halfway between direct worship of elemental nature itself and belief in spirits and divinities inhabiting and animating natural objects and phenomena. The Celts were surrounded by numerous beings of uncertain temper whose goodwill and aid they sought to gain by offerings, supplications, fetishes and the observance of taboos. Classical writers tended to directly equate Celtic deities with their own formalized system of individual, clearly defined gods, but the Celts worshipped broad concepts and qualities under many different names. Each tribe had its own local gods, often based on a superhuman hero-ancestor, and a fertility goddess of life and death with Neolithic origins. Over 400 Celtic god-names have been recorded, around 300 of which occur only once. This symbolic, elliptical approach to religion, with its strong animistic roots, contributed to a preference for outdoor worship and the sanctifying of natural topographical features, such as trees, springs, mountains, rivers, fords, lakes, bogs, stones, caves and islands. Writing of his conquest of Gaul between 58 and 50 BC, Julius Caesar states that the doctrine of the druids was imported into Gaul from Britain. This aristocratic class of priests, seers and judges had an honoured position of privilege and influence within Celtic society. Evolving from earlier shamans, their power was based on the accumulation of a huge, orally transmitted store of knowledge and lore. Druids could read omens, divine the future and maintain correct ritual practice; they had a relationship with the gods but were not in control of them. Many religious customs described by classical writers and defined as Celtic can be glimpsed in the remains and monuments of Neolithic and Bronze Age Britain.

The predominantly warm, dry conditions of the third millennium BC irregularly deteriorated during the Late Bronze Age until, by the start of the Iron Age around 800 BC, the weather was cold and wet. Peat growth had accelerated, wet-loving species were competing with the mixed oak forests of earlier times and some upland and marginal agricultural settlements had been abandoned. In the first century AD, Tacitus described Britain as having a wretched climate with frequent rains and mists, but no extreme cold. These worsening conditions, confirmed by scientific study of faunal and pollen remains, directly affecting everyday life, have been used to explain changes in ritual behaviour during the second millennium BC. Whatever the cause, weapons and hoards became more numerous, and an increased interest was shown in wet conditions: a continuing but more urgent need to be in touch with, and make offerings to, the earth and watery places.

In Switzerland at the Shallows (La Tène) at the eastern end of Lake Neuchâtel, hundreds of votive offerings, including brooches, spears, swords and wooden shields, were found in the peat adjacent to a wooden structure over the River Thièle. The offerings had been displayed on a scaffold or thrown from a bridge. Similar deposits were found next to platforms at Cornaux and Port (Nidau) nearby. Offerings of metalwork were made at Llyn Cerrig Bach (Anglesey) and thrown from a causeway across a marsh at Fiskerton (Lincolnshire). At Flag Fen (Cambridgeshire) over 300 bronzes have been found beside timber uprights. The widely accepted view that metalwork was thrown into rivers and pools has been challenged by Colin Pendleton (*British Archaeology*, March 1995). He discounts the religious significance of wet places in East Anglia, stating that most Bronze Age metalwork believed to have been deposited in water comes from the top of the subsoils underneath the fenland peat and is mainly domestic in origin. Flag Fen provides a dramatic example of metalwork undoubtedly placed in shallow water, over a period of 1,000 years of profound environmental and social change, by people with more than simple domestic concerns.

A wooden model boat containing five pine-wood figures – naked warriors with quartz-pebble eyes, round shields and detachable phalli – came from Roos Carr, north of the Humber estuary, an area famous as a prehistoric boatyard. The model may be connected with the practice of river burial and the transport of souls. On Shuna Island (Argyll), three Bronze Age swords were discovered set upright in the peat. Five upright bronze shields were arranged in a circle in a bog at Beith, southwest of Glasgow. In 1883, a hoard of weapons was discovered while harrowing a potato field near Appleby (Lincolnshire). Broken in antiquity, the bronzes were 200–400 years old before their burial around 750 BC. Fibre marks and accretions on opposed surfaces indicated that they had been laid out in a systematic manner, not in a container or scrap bundle, thus suggesting a funerary or votive rite. Many 'hoards' display ritual elements and may have been 'offerings'. Even the concealment of valuables, out of fear or prudence, involved symbolism and magic to protect the owner and prevent discovery.

In the ancient Mediterranean world, ritual shafts and pits were used to communicate with cthonic deities and as repositories for sacred materials, including the debris from sacrifices. Shafts in the Vendée region of western France contained systematic deposits of pottery, bones and other objects, including, at Le Bernard, an upright cypress stem. Deep shafts of an undoubted sacred nature are found within La Tène-period rectangular earthworks, ritual enclosures called *Viereckschanzen*. At Holzhausen (Bavaria) one shaft had a wooden pole set upright near the bottom. The packing of stones holding the wood in place contained traces of decayed blood, flesh and animal fat, raising visions of sacrifice and ordeal at this stake in the hollow earth. A Bronze Age example was discovered in 1927 while digging for brick clay at Swanwick near Southampton (Hampshire). A post of larch had been set into the bottom of the pit at a depth of 24 feet. When uncovered, the organic fill resembling burnt blood 'stank enough to knock you down', according to the workmen. The site is now occupied by the Civil Aviation Air Traffic Control Centre. An idea of the area's history and the Bursledon Brick Company clay pits may be obtained by visiting the adjacent nature reserve.

Swanwick anticipates the ritual shafts of Iron Age and Roman Britain while carrying echoes of more distant times. The use of shafts and pits features in ancient cults concerned with the ancestors, the abundance of the natural world and the fertility of domestic animals and the fields. Rich soil, good flints and other 'requirements' were placed in pits dug inside Neolithic ritual monuments. At Maumbury Rings in Dorchester (Dorset) forty-five tapering shafts were dug through the bottom of the henge ditch. The cavities, up to 35 feet deep, contained carefully placed stone and bone artefacts layered with deliberate backfill. A practical link with fertility is mentioned by the Elder Pliny, writing in the first century AD. He states that the Britons marled their land in pre-Roman times, sinking pits over 100 feet to get at mixtures of clay, chalk and lime to spread on the fields as manure. In the sixteenth century, dene-holes were used for the same purposes, and in nineteenth-century East Anglia land was 'forced' with dressings of marl or clay obtained from pits in the fields. In Britain a number of deep pits and shafts containing Iron Age and Roman objects have been identified whose unusual contents and methodical layering differentiate them from wells and storage pits casually backfilled with rubbish (Ross, 1968; Wait, 1985). The positively identified pre-Roman ritual shafts are all in England below the Severn–Trent line. A whole oak trunk came from a 51-foot shaft at Rotherfield Peppard (Oxfordshire), along with hazelnuts, deer skulls and complete pots. Three human skeletons were laid out at the bottom of a pit at Greenhithe (Kent); in the fill above were iron objects, plus horse, pig, cow, sheep, deer and bird bones. A shaft in the Belgic cremation cemetery at Aylesford (Kent) was completely full of animal bones. A sixth-century BC example at Ashstead (Surrey) contained layers of ashes, pottery and many animal bones. Pottery shards, ashes, bone fragments, horses' teeth, human bones, a ring, glass and enamel beads, four shale bracelets and twenty bronze ones came from a shaft lined with puddled clay at Cadbury Castle near Tiverton (Devon). At Kelveden (Essex) a chalk figurine had been placed in a niche in a well forming part of a pre-Roman religious site. A shaft lined with oak planks at Ashill (Norfolk) contained over fifty complete pots arranged in layers on beds of hazel and oak twigs with acorns, nuts and leaves, ashes and the bones of deer, cattle and pig. There is evidence for different classes of ritual shaft and changes in their use and contents from Iron Age to Roman times (Wait, 1985).

The Celts perpetuated some ancient customs and showed a superstitious interest in earlier sacred monuments. Burial mounds were considered to be the houses of divine beings, such as the Dagdá and his son, Oengus, inside the megalithic tomb of Newgrange (County Meath), and formed the focal points for ritual and religious games at tribal gatherings and festivals, such as those held at Tara (County Meath) and Emain Macha (Armagh). Aubrey Burl (1981) quotes an old Irish poem in which Celtic warriors dance sunwise inside a stone circle near Tara, to gain strength and protection before going into battle. The *sid(h)* mounds of Ireland and *sithein* of Scotland were regarded as homes of fairies, entrances to the otherworld and scenes of supernatural encounters and testing adventures. Iron Age graves were dug into the Neolithic and Bronze Age ceremonial site at Cairnpapple Hill (West Lothian), which may have been the place known as Medionemeton.

The Celtic word *nemeton* (Latin *nenum*: a clearing within a wood) was used to denote a sacred grove or, more loosely, a tribal sanctuary. It is found as a place-name in Britain and from Spain to Asia Minor, where, according to Strabo, the Galatians held their councils and judged matters of bloodshed at Drunemeton, 'the sacred oak-grove'. The Romans called the spa town of Buxton (Derbyshire) Aquae Arnemetiae, commemorating the goddess of a sacred grove. Tacitus comments on the Roman destruction of 'groves sacred to savage rites' on Anglesey. Dio Cassius describes the fate of Romans and their sympathizers taken captive in Britain during Boudicca's rebellion of AD 60–61: women were tortured in groves dedicated to Andraste, goddess of victory; their breasts were cut off and pushed into their mouths, and their bodies were skewered lengthwise on sharp stakes. Lucan records the discovery of a forest sanctuary by Caesar's axe-men cutting timber before the siege of Marseilles in 49 BC: interlacing branches enclosed a sunless central space where water flowed from dark springs; altars to barbaric gods were heaped with hideous offerings, human blood sprinkled on every tree; the trees were immune to gales and lightning, moved without apparent reason and were devoid of all wildlife; and the images were grim blocks of rough-hewn timber rotted to a ghastly pallor which terrified their devotees.

Although some have expressed scepticism (Rackham, 1994) there is a widespread belief that massive, ancient-looking yews found in many churchyards date from earlier pagan use of the site. Trees did form the focus of some heathen sanctuaries: Christian writers describe trees that were worshipped by Celts and Anglo-Saxons being cursed and destroyed by saints. St Boniface cut down an oak sacred to Thor at Geismar (Germany), using the wood to build a chapel to St Peter. Richard Morris (1989) notes that as late as the eleventh century it was forbidden to own land on which stood a sanctuary centred on a tree. Our name for the yew derives from the Irish *éo*. Sacred yews are mentioned in early Welsh and Irish stories in which heroes and supernatural beings bear tree-names such as 'Son of Yew' and 'Yew Berry'. The name Iona, reputedly a former isle of the druids, comes from a misreading of the Latin *ioua insula*, meaning 'yewy isle'. Along with other evergreens, yew was employed by classical writers as an image of immortality. Christians adopted the symbolism for funerary rituals and hope of the resurrection; yew was also believed to keep the dead from harm. The tenth-century laws of King Hywel Dda of Powys valued the yew of a saint at a pound; a yew of the wood at fifteen pence; an oak at eighty pence; a mistletoe branch at sixty pence.

Yews are notoriously difficult to date, but members of the Conservation Foundation Yew Tree Campaign have been applying modern methods to some of Britain's most revered examples. At Compton Dundon (Somerset), the yew by the south porch of St Andrew's Church was found to be 1,700 years old. The yew at Ffynnon Gwenlais (Dyfed) has been dated to AD 500; it stands at the source of a river and holy well. Excavations at the Chalice Well, Glastonbury, uncovered a yew stump dating to around AD 300 which had been growing at the original ground level of the spring. In Celtic tradition and stories, sacred trees and springs are often linked, and it is still popular to decorate with strips of cloth trees growing near holy wells.

Springs, pools, wells, rivers and their sources were all considered places worthy of worship. So deep-rooted and persistent is the cult of wells that it features throughout this book. In Britain and Gaul, mother goddesses, who also presided over war and prediction, were associated with rivers – appropriate symbols of fertility mixed with powers of destruction. The Brent in Middlesex and the Braint of south-east Anglesey are related to Brigantia, the 'High One'. Other possibilities include the Dee (Deva), the Clyde (Clota), the Severn (Sabrina) and the Wharfe (Verbeia). Rivers were favoured locations for the deposition of fine metalwork. Bronze swords and daggers in scabbards and sheaths, sheet bronze vessels including cauldrons, sheet bronze parade shields and helmets, bronze war trumpets (carnyx), ritual spoons and scoops of bronze, iron swords and daggers all ended up in the water. Accident, misfortune, rivers changing course and erosion of riverside settlements could account for some of the finds, but the high quality and quantity of objects, combined with references in Celtic myths and classical texts to votive offerings in water, suggest a long tradition of deliberate 'loss'. Gerald Wait makes the point that bronze swords are especially found in rivers, and those rivers with swords all flow eastwards: the Nene, Ouse, Tay, Tees, Thames, Trent, Tyne and Witham are the main examples. The concentrations in Lincolnshire and the Thames valley are particularly rich and remarkable. Distributions may be biased, as most finds have been the result of construction and maintenance work, but even large non-east-flowing rivers, such as the Severn and Avon, which have been dredged, have not yet produced votive metalwork (Wait, 1985). River confluences seem to have attracted particular attention, perhaps because they formed tribal boundaries and meeting places. Many objects have been found in the Thames near its junction with the Brent, and an Iron Age shield was deposited at the confluence of the Trent and Soar. Four Roman altars come from County Durham dedicated to Condatis, god of the waters'-meet.

Making a reservoir in 1911 at Llyn Fawr (South Glamorgan) led to the discovery, in the peat of a former lake, of a collection of metal artefacts (mainly bronze) of local and continental manufacture. One single deposition was made of objects of mixed ages, including cauldrons several centuries old. Strabo, quoting Posidonius, describes the Roman consul Caepio, in 106 BC, plundering a mass of metal ingots and coins placed in the temple enclosures and pools of a Celtic sacred site near Toulouse. He says similar treasures existed throughout Celtic lands, the lakes being considered to provide particular inviolability, remaining unprofaned by other tribes. When the Romans conquered an area, they sold such lakes by public auction. According to Eric Wood (1972), in addition to containing votive offerings, sacred lakes can be defined as those having strange properties: persistent traditions and legends give clues as to the former sanctity of such places as Lochmaben (Dumfries), the Silent Pool in Albury (Surrey), Mathern Pill near Chepstow (Gwent) and the village pond at Ewelme (Oxfordshire).

Marshes and lake margins were irresistible to the owners of fine bronzes and ironwork hoards. Late Bronze Age shields (sometimes in groups of three or five) and vessels found in Britain come overwhelmingly from boggy contexts, as do the bronze cauldrons and bowls of the immediately pre-Roman period (Wait, 1985). Nearly all the late prehistoric cauldrons from Ireland were found in bogs (Green, 1986). A circular, ribbed and punched bronze shield was found on the sodden slopes of Moel Siabod (Gwynedd). Bronze cauldrons with votive ironwork came from Carlingwark Loch at Castle Douglas (Dumfries and Galloway), and the peat of a former loch at Blackburn Mill near Cockburnspath (Borders), where one cauldron was inverted over another. Some 2,000 objects, mostly brooches and bracelets, dating from the third to second centuries BC were found in a huge cauldron at the Giant's Spring (Duchov, Czechoslovakia). The Brå cauldron, with a capacity of over 132 gallons, came from a bog in Jutland, as did the Gundestrup cauldron, a silver cult-bowl, laid out, dismantled, in a dry area of the Raevemose bog. It is decorated with images of gods and ceremonies, including a human figure apparently held upside-down over a well or tub by a giant deity. Human sacrifices were made to the Celtic god Teutates by drowning in a container of water. Strabo describes the Cimbri, a Teutonic tribe who sent their most sacred cauldron to the Roman emperor Augustus, slitting the throats of prisoners over such vessels. Cauldrons were both humble domestic utensils and sacred containers. In *Asterix and the Cauldron*, they are used to make onion soup, store treasure and brew magic potion. In Celtic myths cauldrons are invariably magical, capable of inexhaustible supply, rejuvenation and even regeneration of slain warriors.

Cauldrons and weapons were not the only offerings committed to lakes and marshes. Many human bodies have been found in the bogs of Europe, especially in northern Germany and Denmark, where the high degree of preservation because of soil conditions reveals the manner of their deaths. Celtic literature and folklore contain examples of ritual killing; classical historians wrote in outraged terms of the barbaric rites enacted on the fringes of their civilized Mediterranean world; and archaeology has discovered details which are highly suggestive of execution and sacrifice. Human sacrifice was officially ended in the Roman world by a decree of the Senate 97 BC, but the public sacrifice of animals continued as an essential part of Roman religion, with haruspices or 'gut-gazers' employed to interpret the will of the gods from the appearance of livers and entrails. Tollund Man had been kept captive, hanged, cut down, then thrown naked, except for a cap, girdle and leather noose, into the muddy water at the edge of a fen. Borre Fen Man had also been hanged, while Graubelle Man's throat had been cut. A woman in Juthe Fen had been pinned to the peat at each knee and elbow, and by branches across her chest and stomach. A naked, blindfolded young teenage girl came from Windeby in northern Germany: she was held under water by birch branches and a stone, and the left side of her head had been shaved. Tacitus says that the strict moral code of the Germans allowed the husband of an adulterous wife to cut off her hair, strip her, turn her out of the house and flog her through the village (*Germania*, 19). He also describes a group of tribes who worship Mother Earth by the name of Nerthus. Attended by a priest, the goddess lives in a grove on an island in the ocean, travelling to visit her people once a year in a cart veiled by a cloth and drawn by cattle. On returning to the island, the vehicle, the cloth and the goddess herself are washed in a secluded lake by slaves, who are then drowned in the waters of cleansing (*Germania*, 40). Again according to Tacitus (*Germania*, 12), criminals were hanged from trees (traitors and deserters) or plunged into marshes with hurdles to hold their heads under water (cowards, shirkers and sodomites).

The Galatians sacrificed prisoners of war to their gods in the third century BC. Strabo mentions victims ritually killed with arrows or impaled inside temples, much as Boudicca's sacrifices to Andraste. Diodorus Siculus says that the druids stabbed a man above the diaphragm (Strabo says in the back) to foretell the future from his fall, convulsions and spurting blood. The Berne Scholiast on Lucan records that men were sacrificed to the Gaulish god Esus by being hung in trees, then stabbed to draw omens from the direction of the flow of the blood. Sacrifices to Teutates were made by drowning and to Taranis by burning. Tacitus says that in Britain the deities were consulted through human entrails and sacrifices were made for the good of the community. According to Caesar, times of great danger and importance required sacrifice, the gods demanding a human life in order to save the life of another individual or the tribe. If no criminal or prisoner was available, it seems that a 'volunteer' was sought by lot or other means.

The most puzzling example of alleged Celtic sacrifice has been fixed in the modern mind by the *Wicker Image*, an engraving by Aylett Sammes published in 1676, and the 1973 film *The Wicker Man*. These haunting visualizations are based on a description in Caesar of colossal figures of wood with wickerwork limbs filled with human victims (Strabo says humans and animals) burnt alive.

Dedicatory burials or foundation sacrifices were made at Neolithic and Bronze Age monuments in Britain, and this custom was continued by the Celts, particularly inside hillforts. At South Cadbury (Somerset), a young man had been crammed facedown in a pit cut into the back of the inner bank when the rampart was enlarged. A crouched male was found within the bank at Sutton Walls (Hereford and Worcester), and a similar burial had been made in a pit at the junction of two rampart phases at Maiden Castle (Dorset). Foundation burials of possibly deliberately killed infants were made for the Iron Age shrines inside Maiden Castle and at West Hill (north-east of Uley Bury hillfort (Gloucestershire).

As few as 6 per cent of the people who lived at Danebury Ring (Hampshire) had their bones buried in a formal way inside the hillfort. In Britain generally, the remains of around 90 per cent of the Iron Age population are missing: the funeral rite for the majority, therefore, being unknown. Cremation was practised in the Bronze Age, but only the burnt remains of a minority were placed in urns, cists or barrows. Cremation continued in the Iron Age, with ashes probably scattered on water and the land. Ancient inhumation practices continued into the Roman period, especially on the south-west peninsula where burials and deposits of selected bones were placed in cists and stone-lined graves. Low mounds on Ampleforth Moor (North Yorkshire) covered cremations dated to the seventh century BC. At Threlkeld Knotts (Cumbria), small stone piles containing charcoal, situated in Celtic fields beside a rural settlement, may be the results of agricultural clearance or the bases of funeral pyres. By the fifth century BC, the shallow valleys (slacks) of the chalk wolds of south-east Yorkshire were being used to bury most of the adult dead under hundreds of small barrows. Arranged in cemeteries and family clusters, each barrow was surrounded by a rectangular or circular enclosure. Graves were dug in the chalk and gravel for crouched inhumations, usually aligned N-S, unaccompanied, or with basic grave-goods, including brooches and joints of pork. These distinctive Arras-culture burials have similarities with La Tène graves in the Marne region of France. Within the Arras group, a few high-status burials contain a man or woman with a two-wheeled vehicle and such items as pig carcasses, La Tène swords and other weapons, including chain mail, an iron mirror, bronze pins and a decorated bronze canister or 'work box'. The chariot was dismantled, with the wheels laid flat beside the body, used as a 'bed' or propped up in a corner of the burial pit. In addition to chariots, the cemetery at Garton Station contained male burials with weapons, where spears had been thrown into the body lying at the bottom of the grave, then flung into the filling at different levels. Whether this second 'killing' was done out of respect, fear or hatred, to release a spirit or pin a ghost, we cannot say.

In various parts of England and Wales, individual 'warrior burials' are found: adult males laid in shallow, flat graves accompanied by La Tène swords and scabbards, sometimes with spears and shields. A few individuals were buried with a pair of bronze spoons – one of the pair marked with a cross, the other punched with an off-centre hole; these may have been pagan 'priests'. Similar pairs of spoons have been found as ritual deposits in bogs, near springs and under a pile of stones. In the first century BC, the Durotriges of Dorset began to bury their dead in clearly defined cemeteries, with the bodies, lying crouched on the right side, accompanied by complete pots and joints of meat. A distinct group of cremations in south-east England is believed to belong to immigrant Belgic families. Ashes were placed in wheel-turned urns in flat graves along with pots containing food and drink. The group is named after the cemetery at Aylesford (Kent), where a few cremations were placed in large wooden buckets, bound with iron or decorated bronze, accompanied by Italian wine jugs, bronze pans and other costly utensils. A few extremely rich cremations (known as Welwyn burials, after the site in Hertfordshire) were placed in large pits along with exotic and locally made goods used for feasting. The grave pit at Welwyn Garden City contained the cremated remains of a man, accompanied by five amphorae, vessels of silver, bronze and wood, and a board game complete with twenty-four glass pieces. These princely burials, showing the material pleasures and social responsibilities expected in the next world, reveal an increasing sense of personal rather than sacred or tribal wealth. At Folly Lane, St Albans (Hertfordshire), around AD 50, a Celtic aristocrat was laid out in state on a funeral couch inside a timber mortuary house built within a wood-lined pit. After a while the body was taken out and burnt on a pyre along with some of the grave-goods, the hot remains being placed in a cremation pit beside the funerary chamber, which had been ritually destroyed. A ditch formed a 5-acre enclosure around the backfilled pits, its entrance at the west 'guarded' by three human skeletons laid out in one ditch terminal, a deposit of horse and cattle bones in the other. Some fifty years later a Romano-Celtic temple was built on the site of the pyre. Pits just outside the enclosure contained human and animal skulls, and many pots decorated with human faces. The skull of a teenage boy was displayed on a pole in the temple. He had been battered to death and decapitated; the skin had been scraped from the skull but the face was left intact. The excavator, Rosalind Niblett, suggests that the site was used for a pagan cult of the head, eventually Christianized by transferring worship to St Alban, Britain's first recorded Celtic martyr, who was beheaded, possibly in the temple enclosure, in the third century.

The Celts were not unique in valuing the head, but the extent to which its cult ruled their passions is unparalleled. The head was revered as a symbol of the whole, the seat of what made a person individual and divine. Such was its symbolic power that deities were often represented by only a stylized head in wood or stone, or depicted as enlarged heads with tiny trunks and limbs. Heroes of the Irish tales collected heads as trophies of war, stringing them around the necks of their horses and arranging them on stones. The severed head of the Welsh god-king Bran proved an entertaining companion and powerful talisman after his death. Livy reports that the Boii made a gold-mounted cup from the skull of the Roman general Postumius and that the Gauls fastened heads to their saddles and impaled them on spears. According to Diodorus Siculus and Strabo, the heads of respected foes were embalmed in cedar oil to be shown with pride to visitors as family treasures. Pre-Roman shrines in south-east France at Entremont, Glanum, Roquepertuse (all in Provence) and St Blaise (Alpes-Maritimes) contained stone pillars holding human skulls in carved niches. At Entremont, inside the *oppidum* of the Saluvii, the threshold slab to the sanctuary was a reused pillar bearing stylized heads with mouthless faces and closed eyes. From the same shrine came fifteen skulls of fit adult men which had been fastened to a wooden structure with iron nails. One skull had a javelin-head embedded in it and others had been cut from the dried bodies of the battle-dead. Skulls of slain enemies were nailed to house porches and trees. Finds at Bredin Hill (Worcester) and Stanwick (North Yorkshire) suggest severed heads on poles stared down from the gates of hillforts. The use of body parts as signs of victory and warning continued in Britain up to the 1700s. In 1305 Edward I had the head of his Scottish rival Sir William Wallace stuck on a pike on London Bridge; his limbs were displayed at Newcastle, Berwick, Edinburgh and Perth. Skulls preserved in oil were found at the tribal capital of Wroxeter (Shropshire). Human skulls were ritually placed in pits, shafts, wells, sacred lakes and rivers. Many were found in London in the Thames and on the bed of the Walbrook stream (now channelled through a main sewer), along with votive ironwork, coins and pipe-clay figurines.

Tacitus (*Germania*, 9) says:

The Germans do not think it in keeping with the divine majesty to confine gods within walls or to portray them in the likeness of any human countenance. Their holy places are woods and groves, and they apply the names of deities to that hidden presence which is seen only by the eye of reverence.

Diodorus Siculus describes the Gaulish king, Brennus, on seeing images in the temple at Delphi in the early fourth century BC, laughing at the Greeks for believing gods had human form. The majority of Celtic temples and representational sculpture in Britain comes from the Roman period, but the pre-Roman Celts did make images in wood, and there is increasing evidence for shrines and temples built in the Iron Age. A few hill figures and rock carvings may illustrate Celtic gods and concepts in stylized and abstract form. The Long Man of Wilmington, carved on the downs of East Sussex, could be almost any man holding two poles or framed by uprights: a medieval pilgrim, Woden with a spear in each hand, a Roman soldier carrying twin standards, the sun god opening the doors of heaven, a tribal god carrying ceremonial wands, a symbol of Celtic kingship with rods of office. Most hill figures did not survive beyond the Middle Ages. Only tantalizing rumours remain of giants on Plymouth Hoe (Devon) and Shotover Hill (Oxford). The Red Horse(s) of Tysoe (Warwickshire) could have been prehistoric in origin, while the docile nag of Westbury (Wiltshire) may be an eighteenth-century recutting of a Celtic-style horse. On the hillside below the entrance to Wandlebury hillfort in the Gogmagog Hills (Cambridgeshire), T. C. Lethbridge claimed in the 1950s to have discovered huge figures of Celtic gods and goddesses. Normally an archaeologist with a good reputation, on this occasion his methods and findings were extremely controversial, as he conjured a tableau of unique design from a weathered chalk surface riddled with tree roots. There are sixteenth-century and later references to a carved giant inside, or near, the hillfort. As Waendel is one of the names applied to the Long Man of Wilmington, it is just possible Wandlebury gained its name from a similar figure.

The Celts did build sacred enclosures and shrines as well as using groves and other 'natural' settings. The *Viereckschanzen* rectangular earthworks were mentioned earlier when discussing votive shafts. Examples of elongated sub-rectangular sacred compounds come from various parts of Celtic Europe. In France, at Aulnay-sur-Planches (Marne), a ditched enclosure measuring 300 by 50 feet was aligned NE–SW. Dating from the tenth century BC, it contained cremations and a few human burials, including a possible infant sacrifice. A large ox skull found in a pit opposite the south-east-facing entrance may have been a votive burial, or fixed on top of a post. A third-century-BC example at Libenice (Czechoslovakia), 300 by 75 feet, aligned NW–SE, was defined by a continuous ditch. A partly sunken sanctuary at the south-east end revealed pits dug for repeated libations. The sanctuary also contained a standing stone and two close-set post-holes which held wooden images wearing neck-rings. Other pairs of posts stood in the ditch and on either side of the sunken area. A burial near the centre of the enclosure may have been the 'priestess' of this open-air temple. Other pits contained the bones of sacrificed animals and children. Sixth-century-BC enclosures in Germany at the Goldberg and Goloring are similar; a huge central post at Goloring may have been a sacred tree or column. A long and narrow banked earthwork on the Hill of Tara (County Meath) may have been a similar religious enclosure, or ceremonial way approaching the summit complex, which was the seat of the High Kings of Ireland. An undoubted Iron Age ritual complex existed on West Hill, near Uley Bury hillfort (Gloucester). The ditched enclosure contained votive pits and two wooden structures with foundation burials of a baby and infants. The square structure was erected around a large pit which could have held a standing stone, image post or sacred tree. Other deep pits may have held trees or substitutes symbolizing a sacred wood (Woodward, 1992). Iron Age ritual enclosures of varying shapes and sizes have recently been investigated at Colchester and Harlow (both Essex), Hayling Island (Hampshire), and Lancing Ring and Slonk Hill (both Sussex).

Archaeologists did not immediately recognize pre-Roman shrines in Britain. Unless accompanied by obvious religious deposits, the insubstantial remains of ditches and posts were easily confused with domestic structures. In the past, excavators, not always looking carefully below Roman foundations, sometimes missed or destroyed signs of the earlier timber structures. However, things have improved in the last thirty years or so. In 1985, Gerald Wait was able to discuss twenty-five examples from sixteen sites. A timber structure in the third-century-BC settlement under Heathrow Airport (Middlesex) appears to anticipate the standard Romano-Celtic temple ground plan of two concentric squares with aligned entrances. It had a small central 'cella' surrounded by an 'ambulatory', both with entrances facing east. The outer wall or fence may be earlier than the inner, which is of a different build; a Roman-period shrine may have been added to a square religious enclosure of the sort found at Danebury Ring (Hampshire). Excavations behind the Ark Hotel at Frilford (Oxfordshire) discovered a unique form of temple: a deep, wide penannular ditch with a western entrance and six posts arranged in a double N–S row. An iron ploughshare was buried in one of the post-holes and a miniature bronze sword and shield in a square pit. At Worth (Kent) a Romano-Celtic temple had been built over an earlier shrine indicated by four post-holes, brooches and three model shields of La Tène design.

The shrines recognized so far are located in England, south of the Midlands. Mainly associated with occupation, showing a marked preference for tribal boundary areas and political centres such as major hillforts, they played a part in trade and social integration as well as religion. Four small rectangular shrines were situated on the false crest near the centre of Danebury Ring hillfort. Three with plank walls and gabled thatched roofs stood either side of a pathway branching from the main road across the fort; the fourth, probably a fenced enclosure, lay astride the path. The shrines all faced the eastern gateway, from where they would have appeared on the skyline. Shrines at Maiden Castle (Dorset) stood at the end of a roadway leading from the eastern gateway. The overwhelming majority of shrine entrances face eastwards, suggesting that to approach from or look towards that direction had important symbolic or ritual significance: perhaps the deity or priest needed to see the first glimpse of dawn or moonrise.

Iron Age shrines provided a focus for cult activity, which mainly took place in the open. Although it might have been possible to squash around thirty people into the larger ones, a shrine was an intimate private place for a priest-attendant, supplicant and the presence of a deity. The ground area increased in the Roman period to accommodate the more public ceremonies, but the majority of worshippers still participated outside in the temple precincts.

In northern Britain there are very few structural remains which can be directly linked with pre-Roman Celtic religion. In Ballachulish (Highland), a female figurine of oak with agate eyes was found lying in the peat, surrounded by remains from a wickerwork hut or wattle-walled enclosure.

Flag Fen, Cambridgeshire

Below: A modern lagoon constructed over the central part of the artificial island to preserve its timbers. The model island and alignment give an impression of the original arrangement.

Excavations on the eastern outskirts of Peterborough have recovered over 330 bronze artefacts, all deliberately deposited in shallow water beside timber uprights. The rows of posts ran for over half a mile in a straight line NW–SE across the seasonally flooded basin of Flag Fen. An artificial island was built, using over a million timbers, near the centre of a permanent lagoon in the lowest area of the basin. On its way southeast from Fengate, the alignment crossed over the platform before ending on dry land at Northey. The post-alignment followed the course of Neolithic ditches and a Bronze Age droveway through fields flooded as the rising sea level blocked river outfalls. Begun around 1300 BC, the alignment was maintained and repaired for at least 400 years. It was 33 feet wide, made up of four main rows but up to seven lines of posts, with a walkway of planks laid between two of the rows. Successive floor levels were constructed as the water level rose, sand, fine gravel and wood-chips being spread on the slippery surfaces. Wattle-and-daub partitions between uprights closed off parts of the alignment. The earliest posts were of alder but increasingly oak, brought from up to 12 miles away, was used. Holes and joints showed some timbers had come from earlier short-lived structures, perhaps dismantled

because of the flooding. Weapons and ornaments, but very few tools, dating from 1400 to 300 BC were placed among the posts and in a band 67–98 feet wide along the southern, landward side; hardly anything was found on the fenward side. All the objects had been damaged before being placed in the water: bronze swords, rapiers, pins, brooches, rings and miniature wheels were bent or broken; the wooden shafts of spearheads were snapped. Over 1,000 years of deposition the style of objects changed but the rite did not, and offerings continued to be made for over 500 years after the posts had rotted off. The initial flooding was a mixed blessing: settlements and field systems became unusable, but at the margins the river silt – in a natural version

Right: *Part of the Northey end of the post-alignment preserved beneath sprays of refrigerated water in the exhibition hall. A mural giving 'Bronze Age' views in all four directions and an eerie soundscape, including appropriate species, greatly add to the appreciation of this remarkable structure.*

Inset left: *Inside the excavation tent, August 1995. A massive 3,000-year-old timber built into the post-alignment overlooks a deliberately formed pool containing a dog skeleton. The high number of dog remains from the alignment and platform, and the nature of their deposition, suggest some kind of cult practice.*

of the medieval system of controlled water-meadows – would have limed and enriched the winter-flooded pasture ready for summer grazing. The new lagoon supported an abundance of fish, eels and edible water-birds, including pelicans.

By around 900 BC, when the replacement of rotted posts ceased, the flood-meadows were too wet even for summer grazing. The alignment seems more than a simple wetland track-way, although it did give access to the ceremonial platform and provided a useful causeway across seasonal floods. It may have been used for display, or as a sacred 'bridge' maintaining a revered earthwork alignment – perhaps an ancient route of symbolic or economic importance. The structure is massive enough to have been a palisade, an attempt to hold back the waters, or protect, placate and proclaim ownership over a valued resource. Were the ashes of the dead sprinkled from the walkway while their belongings were ceremonially broken and placed in the otherworld beneath the water? Did the living gain status and reassurance by offering valuables to a magical lake – revered for its associations with fertility and death – where they lay beneath the shape-shifting surface, visible from this world but inviolate.

Wilsford Shaft, Amesbury, Wiltshire

The shaft lies beneath the surface of a field rendered featureless by modern agriculture, a mile south-west of Stonehenge. Investigation of the circular bank and central hollow of a pond barrow uncovered a well-like shaft cut through the chalk with antler picks and will power to a depth of 100 feet. The shaft was 6 feet in diameter, its rough faces dressed by a metal axe. Dug in short vertical sections, each one checked and corrected by template and plumbline, it may have taken a small team a year of dangerous and exacting labour to excavate the chalk.

Runnymede Bridge, Egham, Surrey

Another Late Bronze Age community flirting dangerously with rising water levels was situated by the south bank of the River Thames at Egham, south of its present course. This extensive settlement specialized in metalworking and trading goods between central England and continental Europe. Boats moored up against a timber-pile wharf and landing stage. Votive offerings may have been made to the water, as more metalwork ended up in the river than can be accounted for by carelessness and accident – perhaps a portion of each cargo was dedicated to the appropriate gods. Deteriorating weather conditions and poor drainage caused the final flooding and abandonment of the site by around the eighth century BC. The complex was investigated in the 1950s and 1970s during the construction of the A30 and M25 road bridges.

Digging stopped when a water-bearing fissure was hit, causing the bottom of the shaft to flood. Interpretation of this tantalizing and enigmatic site hinges on whether striking water was the result of brilliant technique and guesswork or unforeseen chance. Study of environmental indicators such as insects, pollens and seeds preserved in waterlogged deposits at the base of the shaft, along with other organic material including remains of wooden buckets and plant ropes, led to the conclusion that it was deliberately dug as a well to water cattle and sheep which were fed close by. A wooden structure was at the well-head, situated in an agricultural landscape of grazed grassland with fields of barley, emmer wheat and flax. The biological material gave no definite evidence for ritual, but the archaeological conclusion was that the shaft, dug for non-material purposes, was abandoned unfinished when water was accidentally encountered. The difficulties of accurately predicting water-bearing cavities in chalk, the quality and unnecessary sophistication of the work, the existence of similar shafts with ritual deposits, and the possibly votive nature of amber beads, bone pins, a shale ring, butchered bones, fleeces, pot shards and an ox skull – all from near the bottom – seem to edge the purpose of the shaft in a ritual direction. The process of making the shaft-well may have been far more important than what was produced. Other shafts could be lurking beneath some of the twenty-five or so pond barrows distributed among the Wessex culture cemeteries around Stonehenge.

Cairnpapple Hill, Torphichen, West Lothian

This hilltop near Edinburgh has been used as an observatory and ceremonial centre since 3000 BC. It is the site of a cremation cemetery, a henge monument, a stone circle, burials and cairns. Four rectangular full-length graves, dug between the henge ditch and holes of the demolished stone circle, reveal Iron Age use of the monument. Modern white gravel distinguishes the later graves from stone holes and a Beaker burial. The excavator, Stuart Piggott, has suggested Cairnpapple as Medionemeton – the 'middle sanctuary' – of Roman times, described in the *Ravenna Cosmography* (a list of Roman place-names compiled by a seventh-century cleric of Ravenna) as located on the neck of land between the Clyde and Forth estuaries. Bar Hill to the west, on the line of the Antonine Wall, is also a contender for the site of the Celtic sanctuary.

St Anne's Well, Buxton, Derbyshire

The Romans established a settlement on the valley floor around mineral springs yielding two different types of water. They called it Aquae Arnemetiae – 'waters of she who dwelt over against the sacred grove' – after a Celtic sanctuary and

goddess/priestess connected with the spa waters. This well is now named for the mother of the Virgin Mary, but the original dedication may have been to the mother goddess Anu, or Santan, the holy fire. Medieval pilgrims sought cures at the wells, as did Mary Queen of Scots, who praised the 'milkwarm waters'. Roman baths lie under the nineteenth-century Crescent; coins found in the well date from Roman times up to the seventeenth century, when the well chapel was abandoned.

The present well-head stands opposite the Crescent at the foot of the Slopes, Palladian-style gardens laid out around 1818. Over 250,000 gallons of water a day flow from a mile underground, at a constant temperature of 82°F. The warm, slightly salty, soda-tasting liquid was good on hands and palate on a frosty morning. Many people stopped on their way to work to fill plastic bottles with this healthful and valued 'living water'.

Castell Henllys, Newport, Dyfed

An imaginative reconstruction of a shrine outside a defended Celtic settlement. Wooden images, one of a Cernunnos type with stag horns and a torc, have been placed at a natural spring along with offerings, fetishes and strips of cloth.

Croft Ambrey, Leominster, Hereford and Worcester

Mistletoe grows on a number of trees, most commonly apple and crab, and very rarely on oak. Pliny the Elder said that the Gaulish druids considered mistletoe growing on oak a gift of god. On the sixth day of the moon, a white-robed priest ascended the tree with a 'golden' (?bronze) sickle to cut the mistletoe, which fell into a white cloak. Two white bulls were sacrificed, a banquet held and prayers and thanks offered. The druids called mistletoe 'all-heal', believing that it could make barren animals fertile and was an antidote to all poisons. In the seventeenth century, the astrologer-physician Nicholas Culpeper was recommending misseltoe (*sic*) as a cure for nervous ailments and to drive out humours from the body.

By tradition, the apple was the fruit of the Tree of Knowledge, and golden apples grew in a magic orchard guarded by the nymphs of evening (the Hesperides). In Irish legends a tub of sacred otherworld apples is often possessed by a Celtic goddess. The Welsh word for apple is *afel* ('f' is pronounced 'v') hence Avalon, the 'Apple Island' of Arthurian romance, used widely in literature and poetry as a symbol for paradise and the next world. Religious ceremonies took place in the southern annexe of Croft Ambrey hillfort. Animal sacrifices supported on stakes were made on a terrace, later covered by a large flat-topped mound.

Wistman's Wood, Dartmoor, Devon

These stunted trees form one of the best examples in Britain of high altitude oak-wood. In difficult conditions oaks grow very slowly: a tree cut down in 1868 was about 168 years old but only 9 inches in diameter. The largest living trees could easily be 400 years old or more. The origin of this ancient woodland is a mystery, as is the fact that the trees are mainly pendunculate rather than the sessile oaks found elsewhere on Dartmoor. Whatever their age and history, the contorted trees with gnarled and swollen limbs seem a force to be reckoned with.

The ancient oaks are becoming hollow – 'dying' but retaining their own life while supporting others. They are host to mistletoe, and beards of lichen hang from their jagged twigs, while mosses, ferns, bilberries, young rowans and oaks germinate and grow on the seedbeds of their horizontal boughs – venerable ancestors covered and surrounded by their diverse and numerous children. The trees possess a deliberate, enduring power; they split and engulf granite outcrops with their penetrating roots, pushing away earth and stones as tensed limbs expand, bend, arch and flex. Wistman's Wood is not a druidic grove, but it is a suitable location to experience the character and personalities of ancient oaks, and to contemplate what can make a place holy.

Overton,
Wrexham, Clwyd

The yews in St Mary's churchyard were described by Thomas Pennant in the eighteenth century as one of the seven wonders of Wales. Most date from the late fourteenth century, when the present church was begun, while others are from the 1830s. Based on growth-ring evidence, this gnarled and hollow specimen, chained and propped beside the north-west gate, appears to have been here for around 2,000 years, making it certainly older than the first Christian use of the site in the seventh century.

Sherwood Forest Country Park,
Edwinstowe, Nottinghamshire

Birkland Wood contains several hundred oaks, survivors of the 21,000 recorded in 1609. Some stand stark and completely dead, while others are of the form known as stag-head. The head dies back to keep in balance with the roots. A smaller, healthier crown develops below the dead boughs which do not rot off. For the Celts and the druids in particular, the oak was the principal sacred tree. Its ability to resist decay, obtain a great age (the nearby Major Oak is around 800 years old) and be simultaneously dead and alive must have been valued and wondered at. The antlered heads are reminiscent of Cernunnos, the stag-horned father god and divine ancestor of the Gauls. Depicted as 'lord of the animals, nature and prosperity', sitting in a 'Buddhic' pose with his usual attributes of neck-torc, ram-headed serpent and a stag, he was one of the few Celtic deities to achieve a wide distribution and reasonably consistent form. An example of shape-shifting, his origins lie in Stone Age cave paintings showing hunters and shamans wearing the horns and skins of quarry and totem animals for magical purposes. He lingers on in such figures as Herne the Hunter of British folklore and the horned one, despised, demonized and perpetuated by the Christian Church.

Tarren Deusant,
Llantrisant, Mid-Glamorgan

This pagan cult site is a good example of Celtic sensitivity to an unusual arrangement of natural features. A spring issuing from the base of a sombre cliff has gained significance from the presence of a startling, drop-shaped stone, trapped in a block of mudstone in the rock face to the south. Carvings surround the orange tear, including at least eight human faces. When Lhuyd (*Parochialia* III) recorded the name and site in 1696, the 'Rock of Two Saints' had only 'two persons engraved'. Two carvings on the left have the incised eyebrows and slit mouths characteristic of some Celtic cult heads. The association of human heads with sacred waters is a common theme in Celtic tales. Although impossible to date, Tarren Deusant has the look and 'feel' – simultaneously benign and threatening – of a genuine pre-Christian cult site.

Chalice Well Gardens, Glastonbury, Somerset

The Chalice Well stream flows through modern gardens in the valley between Glastonbury Tor and Chalice Hill. Earlier names include Chalk Well, signifying a limestone or cold well, and Blood Spring, because of the iron-red waters which became associated with the blood of Christ. Some modern visitors consider the flow to be the womb-waters of the earth goddess: the regenerative blood of birth and menstruation, charged with power by proximity to the Tor. It is possible that the Celts also saw the therapeutic waters of chalybeate springs as the gift of a goddess. Finds from the buried ground surface around the original spring, 12 feet below the present well-head, show that it was visited long before Roman times. A yew stump from the same level may be the remains of a processional avenue approaching the well from the east.

Newtondale Spring, Pickering, North Yorkshire

A chalybeate healing well of ancient use, situated near the bottom of a rock face where a flow of mineral-rich water emerges from the body of the earth.

Sancreed,
West Penwith, Cornwall

The iron produces orange staining and a tangy, rusty-metal taste, while the high lime content petrifies the vegetation on the hillside below. In the eighteenth century this deposit was sold as 'marl' to sweeten and invigorate the acid moorland fields of Goatland farmers, and the water was recommended for restoring weak joints and limbs. A few blocks of stone remain in place from the cisterns and well house built in the 1600s.

On Chapel Downs to the south-west of Sancreed Parish Church is a ruined chapel and ancient baptistery – an underground chamber containing a well reached by steep, narrow steps. The spring and chamber are almost certainly pre-Christian in origin. This is a magical combination of a spring and entrance to the otherworld: a place for votives and vigil, for contact with the spirits of earth and water. In addition to the spirits, the well has gained a guardian saint, but offerings are still hidden between the stones.

Schiehallion,
Tayside

The 3,547-foot peak of Schiehallion watches over the Tummel–Rannoch valley, with Loch Tay to the south and the wilds of Rannoch Moor to the west. It is Sidh Chailleann – 'sacred place (or fairy mound) of the Caledonians' – a good example of a Celtic tribe, identifying with territorial and landscape features, having a sacred mountain much the same as the Aboriginals of North America and Australia. The mountain is a shape-shifter: from the north it is a long, humpbacked ridge cloaked in cloud, but from Loch Rannoch, to the north-west, it is revealed as pyramidal and sharp-pointed.

Ingleborough Hill, Ingleton, North Yorkshire

The distinctive millstone grit cap of Ingleborough Hill rises from a limestone landscape shaped and scarred by ice, a land of mines, caverns, rushing water, moors criss-crossed by prehistoric tracks, Roman roads and medieval droveways. A massive wall of blocks and slabs defends the summit plateau, where there are the remains of many circular huts. At 2,370 feet, this is England's highest hillfort: a major centre of the Setantii tribe of Brigantia. It may be the place named Rigodunum – 'royal stronghold' – in Roman documents, and one of the last forts to yield to the legions. The Brigantes – the 'High Ones' – took their name from Brigantia, the goddess they worshipped. It is not clear if Ingleborough was a continuously occupied 'town' or a royal site used periodically for ceremonial and religious functions. The hill is the perfect landscape expression of the power and toughness of a goddess and her people who offered such stubborn resistance to the Romans.

Left and above: *Shape-shifting scenery. Two views of Schiehallion, Tayside.*

River Thames, Syon Reach, Brentford, Middlesex

A bronze sword came from Syon Reach and a further six from Brentford, where flats rise high and Brigantia's river meets the Thames. Collections of Celtic metalwork have been retrieved from the river at over twenty locations in the London area, with further examples from Surrey, Middlesex, Berkshire and Oxfordshire. Especially noteworthy are the magnificent bronze parade shield, cauldron and swords from Battersea; bronze shields and swords from Wandsworth, and the Waterloo horned bronze helmet. A cult of the deified Thames is suspected, perhaps on a par with the 'Mother Ganges' of the Hindus, with votive offerings being made in the vicinity of bridges and regular crossing-places where mortals were at the mercy of the gods. Fords and crossings are darkly symbolic in Celtic myths – places of danger and passing; of battles and single combat; of human trickery and supernatural attack, where a doomed hero sees his bloodstained clothes being washed by the 'Hag of the Ford'. At the Thames near Brentford in AD 43 the British, led by Caratacus and Togodumnus, were soundly defeated by the advancing Romans.

River Witham, Tattershall Bridge, Lincolnshire

In 1768 a boar's head, made of hammered bronze held together by solder, was dredged up from the Witham at Tattershall Ferry. It is the terminal to a carnyx: a Celtic war trumpet topped with an animal head. Illustrated held aloft on coins, reliefs and the Gundestrup cauldron, carnyxes were blown at sacrifices and contributed to the terrifying din made by the Celts before battles. A remarkable number of fine Iron Age metalwork objects have come from the river between the A153 crossing at Tattershall and Lincoln, 18 miles to the north-west. Finds include the famous Witham parade shield, bearing the impression of a stylized boar; iron swords and daggers with bronze and iron scabbards; and two bronze swords. The Gaulish raven goddess, who was the consort of the god Sucellos – 'Good Striker' – was called Nantosuelta, a name meaning 'winding river'.

Llyn Cerrig Bach, Anglesey

Between 1942 and 1945 the eerie landscape of outcrops and marshy pools at Llyn Cerrig Bach was extensively remodelled during the construction and expansion of Valley RAF Station. Peat, dragged from the area of a former lake on the northern perimeter of the aerodrome, was spread across the coastal runway site to consolidate windblown sand. Many domestic animal bones and around 175 pieces of Celtic metalwork thrown into the marshy lake were recovered from the peat. Details of the discovery are confusing; the area has been quarried, blasted, levelled and two small artificial lakes formed in the dredged and partly backfilled basin. Survey

work in 1995 by Philip Macdonald and Tim Young suggested a strip of land, now dividing the modern lakes, had formed an Iron Age 'island' in the marsh. Finds came from the narrowest area between the island and a rock cliff at the edge of the bog. If votive offerings were displayed or thrown from a causeway connecting these two points, the rite would match other sacred lakes and springs in Britain and on the Continent. The deliberately damaged objects are predominantly martial in character: eleven swords, two complete and in scabbards; a dagger; iron spearheads; parts of one or two parade shields; pieces of horse harness; remains of up to twenty-two light, two-wheeled chariots (mainly iron tyres); pieces of two sheet-bronze cauldrons; a broken curved bronze trumpet from Ireland; spirals of bronze ribbon decoration from ceremonial ash wands; five iron currency bars or symbolic ploughshares; two gang-chains of iron, each with neck-rings to hold five captives; plus miscellaneous fragments and tools such as tongs and sickles. The swords, shields and harness date from the second century BC; the other objects vary in date up to the first century AD. They come from several different parts of Britain, but there is a special link with the immigrant Belgic tribes of southern England who used the distinctive type of gang-chain found at Llyn Cerrig Bach. They took captives from other tribes in Britain, selling them as slaves to the Romans.

In AD 60 Suetonius Paulinus invaded Anglesey, transporting his infantry across the Menai Strait in flat-bottomed boats while his cavalry waded and swam. Tacitus makes it clear that the island was considered a serious threat to the Romans, as it was taking in political refugees from the south and 'feeding the native resistance'. It may also have been an important religious centre. Tacitus does not claim Anglesey as the seat of druidism, but it is possible that druids fleeing there were encouraging a sense of nationalism and united action among the usually fragmented, quarrelsome tribes. He draws attention to druids in the battle on the Anglesey shore 'calling down terrible curses' on Roman soldiers, and says of the island priests that 'their religion enjoins them to drench their altars with the blood of prisoners, and to find the will of the gods by consulting the entrails of human beings'. Tacitus also describes the seeking out and destruction by the Romans of sacred groves on the island. No examples of metalwork later than AD 60 were found at Llyn Cerrig Bach, which could be seen as one huge offering in a last desperate attempt to stir the gods, or put valuable and sacred objects beyond reach as the Romans fought through north Wales, advancing upon the island retreat. This would have required the giving up of many 'heirlooms' as donations to the war effort by warriors and households, or the removal of a previously inviolate hoard accumulated in another sacred, but vulnerable, location. Caesar, speaking of the Gauls, says 'after a victory [they] sacrifice such living things as they have captured and all other booty they gather together in one place. In many tribal areas heaps of such things can be seen piled up in sacred precincts.' Strabo says that sacred pools were also used. The objects at Llyn Cerrig Bach were uncorroded, suggesting that they were put immediately under water and did not accumulate in an outdoor sanctuary.

It looks as though for 150–200 years repeated offerings were made at a remote but widely known site of great sanctity (Lynch, 1991). Deposition of so many individual chariot wheels may give a clue to the cult. From the Bronze Age, wheels were used as solar symbols – the hub the sun, the spokes the rays, the rim the surrounding nimbus (Green, 1986) – and thrown into water, where the sun appeared to float. Many miniature wheels were found submerged at Flag Fen, and 200 came from the Loire, near Orléans. Wheel symbols protected armour and symbolized Taranis the 'Thunderer', a Gaulish mixture of Jupiter and Mars, a sky-horseman-warrior with dominion over death. Did the chariot wheels at Llyn Cerrig Bach honour a local god of war, who fought with thunderbolts and lightning?

The start of lavender growing on a commercial
scale in Norfolk led to the discovery of the
Snettisham treasure. Lavender was certainly
grown by the Romans, who burnt it in honour
of their gods. They also used lavender as an
antiseptic and insect-repellent, and to scent
their public baths.

Norfolk Lavender Ltd, Heacham, Norfolk

At Snettisham in 1948 six torcs were turned up while deep-ploughing a field to plant lavender. Since then 175 whole and partial examples have been found, with precious metal ingots and 234 coins buried in fourteen hoards of scrap and bullion. Torcs may have been used as a form of currency, but some of the better ones must have been valued as personal or ceremonial objects. Dio Cassius describes the Icenian queen Boudicca as wearing a great gold necklace. Some of the finer pieces were carefully concealed in deeper pits beneath the false subsoil bottoms of shallow pits containing less valuable items. All the objects were buried on one occasion around 70 BC. Diodorus Siculus describes large amounts of gold placed openly as dedications to the gods in sanctuaries throughout Gaul. Caesar states that many sacred places in Gaul contained mounds of votive offerings held inviolable on pain of death. It is possible that Snettisham was a sacred treasury of the Iceni, similar to the treasure of Toulouse plundered by the Romans. Whoever buried the Snettisham treasure thought it at risk. Archaeological excavations also traced a deep V-shaped ditch, dated by coins to AD 80, enclosing an area of 20 acres with the hoards near its centre. If the date for the ditch is correct, someone, Celt or Roman, went to a lot of trouble to enclose the known, or suspected, site of a 150-year-old ritual, or accidentally included the hoards within a ditched area the size of a small town. No signs of occupation or religious use of the site were found. In February 1996 a Radio 4 news item featured an aristocratic family forced to flee East Germany on the communist take-over. Before leaving they buried their gold and silver treasure in two pits deep in a wood, returning after reunification to find it undisturbed.

Castle Loch, Lochmaben, Dumfries and Galloway

Lochmaben was the lake of the 'Divine Youth' Mabon, a native Celtic god, worshipped in Roman times as Maponus. Dedications on altars from the Hadrian's Wall area equate him with Apollo, the sun god whose healing, hunting and musical aspects he shares. Apollo was sometimes worshipped in Britain as 'Hound Lord', keeper of sacred dogs which could heal by licking. In the story of Culhwch and Olwen, the earliest Arthurian tale in Welsh, Mabon is described as Mabon son of Modron (son, son of mother), who was taken away three nights old from his mother and imprisoned in a sinister fortress, whereabouts unknown. He is the only person who can act as houndsman to hunt the boar Twrch Trwyth – one of the many interlinked, seemingly impossible tasks Arthur and his companions are set by the giant Ysbadden, who hopes to prevent his daughter, Olwen, marrying Culhwch.

Mabon is finally located and freed with the help of a magical salmon, the oldest living creature, who is traced by finding other magical animals, each one more ancient than the previous. The series of wearying and convoluted tasks is eventually successfully completed, the giant is killed and the lovers wed. This complicated medieval adventure is believed to contain the distorted remnants of the cult story of an ancient god.

Clochmaben Stone, Gretna, Dumfries and Galloway

A massive glacial erratic, situated just east of the Kirtle Water on raised ground overlooking the Solway Firth and the mountains of Cumbria. This granite boulder, and its smaller companion in the hedge, formed part of a stone circle removed in the early 1800s to gain half an acre of agricultural land. The megalith fell over in the 1970s. Charcoal sealed in the underlying hole gave a carbon-14 date of around 3200 BC – a time when stone axes from Cumbrian screes were traded throughout Britain and large, open stone circles were used for seasonal gatherings and religious festivals. Situated on an important river crossing between England and Scotland, the site became a recognized place of assembly. Roman information, repeated in the seventh-century *Ravenna Cosmography*, places the Locus Maponi, a tribal meeting-place and cult centre of the god Mabon, in this area. Although Neolithic in origin, the location is typical of a Celtic sacred place: by a crossing-place at the confluence of three rivers, overlooking a powerful, dangerous estuary marking a tribal boundary. An ancient place for markets, judgements and trysting, local gatherings were held here until fairly recently. Between 1754, when clandestine marriages were made illegal in England, and 1940, the Old Smithy at nearby Gretna Green was famous for runaway romances. A legal marriage could be obtained without a licence, banns or priest, by making declarations in front of the blacksmith.

Clackmannan Stone, Clackmannan, Stirling

Another tribal stone and rallying point may be seen at Clackmannan, near Alloa. The Clach Mannan – Stone of the Manau – named after the local group of Iron Age Celts, is a natural whinstone boulder. It was placed on top of a monolith in the town centre in 1833 after being kept for many years in Clackmannan Tower. The stone reputedly came from below Lookaboutye Brae, just south of the town, where it marked a sacred place and point of assembly for the local tribes. In ancient Greece the omphalos or navel stone at Delphi was held to mark the centre of the world. Ceremonial use of similar domed boulders, rather than standing stones, is well known in the Celtic world, especially in Ireland, where the two best examples, at Turoe and Castlestrange, are decorated with La Tène curves and swirls.

Lookaboutye Brae, Clackmannan

The original site of the Stone of the Manau may have been near the house on the left of the road, in the fields at the foot of rising ground now leading up to the town.

Wren's Egg, Wigtown, Dumfries and Galloway

A large granite boulder laid by a glacier – not a traumatized wren – on the low ridge north-west of Blairbuie Farmhouse. Two small standing stones downhill to the east were once thought to be the remains of a pair of concentric circles centred on the egg. Recent work on the site did not confirm this idea, but traces of Bronze Age activity were found at the bases of the standing stones. There is no evidence for it, but the Wren's Egg is just the sort of strange stone the Celts were attracted to use.

Derwentwater, Cumbria

The widest of the Cumbrian lakes shares with Lochmaben the rare vendace fish and an unconfirmed reputation of ancient sanctity. Its Celtic name, Derwent, derives from the same word for oak tree as the term druid. Geoffrey Ashe (1978) believes Derwentwater to be the most likely original location for the Arthurian story of Lancelot, who was taken away from his parents to be raised by the Lady of the Lake on a water 'fair and broad'. Is this based on a memory of pagan priestesses, with an island sanctuary on a broad lake surrounded by many oaks?

Posidonius describes the Celtic priestesses of an island shrine off the mouth of the Loire, while Pomponius Mela speaks of nine with magic powers who dwell on the Ile de Sein, south-west of the tip of Brittany. Sunlit St Herbert's Isle, seen here from Surprise View, is named after the seventh-century hermit who sought solitude and died there. It is also 'Owl Island' of Beatrix Potter's *Tale of Squirrel Nutkin*, where the red squirrels go for six days to gather hazelnuts – the Celtic nuts of wisdom.

Lindow Common, Wilmslow, Cheshire

A peat-shredding machine on Lindow Moss in August 1984 revealed the right foot and lower leg of the bog body now popularly known as Pete Marsh – a muscular young man of twenty-five or so, 5 feet 6 inches tall, in good health except for intestinal worms and a little arthritis. He had dark brown hair, a clipped moustache and a beard stained red by decomposing moss; his nails were manicured and unmarked by hard labour; his blood group was type O. He was alive in the stressful early years of the Roman occupation – an ordinary young man maybe, but Anne Ross (Ross and Robbins, 1989) believes he may have been a member of the Celtic aristocracy, a druid even, and a not totally unwilling victim of a ritual killing.

He was struck twice on the head from behind, strangled, stabbed in the throat and pushed into a bog pool, where he lay crouched in the rapidly forming peat for nearly 2,000 years. The blows to the head knocked bone fragments into the skull cavity and drove his jaws together, chipping a tooth. Probably unconscious, but still alive, a thin strand of sinew was placed around his throat and tightened with a stick to break his neck while his bulging jugular vein was stabbed to release its blood in a powerful spurt. He went naked into the mire except for an arm-band of fox fur. His gut contained a few grains of mistletoe pollen – a plant sacred to the druids. Shortly before his death he had eaten a small amount of bread, some of which had been deliberately charred. The lack of signs of a struggle or restraint have been taken to signify a calm acceptance of his fate. Celtic folk tales and seasonal games preserve the custom of choosing by lot using small loaves, the 'victim' being the one who draws the charred or blackened bread.

In 1987 another naked male came from the same bog. Dated to the early Roman period, he had been beheaded aged around twenty-two, after a last meal of cereals and hazelnuts. He had two thumbs on his right hand and a body decorated with a blue-green mineral-based paint. Caesar describes the Celts painting them-selves with *vitrum* – usually interpreted as the vegetable dye woad – before religious rituals or going naked into battle. This was believed to give magical protection, much as the war paint of Native Americans or the tattoos of the Scythians.

This educational pond, with dipping platform for collecting specimens, is in the Lindow Common Nature Reserve, a mile north-east of where Pete Marsh was found. The pool and platform resemble Celtic arrangements for making votive offerings in sacred lakes and bogs. A visit to the common gives a good idea of the Iron Age landscape of mire pools, bog vegetation and birch scrub in which the killings took place.

Danebury Ring, Stockbridge, Hampshire

For the people of Danebury, disturbing the earth in any way was usually accompanied by ritual and offering. Sometime before the fort was started in the sixth century BC, an arc of deep pits was dug along the north-east contour of the hill, just beyond the line chosen later for the ramparts. Massive central posts – possibly idols – were fixed into the pits on top of dog burials and the bones of a wide variety of animals. Human bones were used as protective charms, or thanks offerings to the earth gods, in the grain storage pits dug inside the fort; a particular interest was shown in pelvic girdles and male skulls. When this northern rampart was being enlarged, three male foundation sacrifices were carefully buried at the bottom of the

quarry area, inside the fort to the left. They are significantly different from the other, mainly disarticulated, human burials inside the fort. 'Criminals' were flung into ditches and pits to lie in a heap with the rubbish, their bodies weighted down with stones to stop the spirits rising. The more favoured dead were excarnated: their bodies exposed outside the fort, the flesh decaying in the open air, allowing their spirits to start the journey to the otherworld or rebirth.

Cadbury Castle, South Cadbury, Somerset

The body of a young man was buried in this length of the upper rampart in the first century AD, when the hillfort was refurbished as a 'town' of the Durotriges tribe. He is believed to have been a foundation sacrifice to propitiate the 'god' of the old work and to protect the new rampart built above him – an attempt to fix a guardian spirit in place. At the same time a small wooden shrine was in use near the centre of the interior. It had an inner sanctum with a porch or veranda on the east.

Outside, some twenty sacrificial burials of pigs and lambs, but mainly newly born calves, had been made. A collection of 'weapon burials' just to the north suggested 'warrior' and 'peasant' offerings had been made in separate areas on opposite sides of the approach to the shrine.

Left: *Looking south-
wards over farmland
reconstituted after gravel
extraction in the valley
bottom. The centre of the
Iron Age complex was
near where the trackway
meets the quarry road.*

Wetwang Slack, Great Driffield, East Yorkshire

Archaeological excavations have accompanied the gravel extraction advancing through the slacks (shallow valleys) of Garton and Wetwang, north-west of Great Driffield. A series of settlements and Arras-culture burials, including chariots, have been discovered strung out along an Iron Age roadway and boundary earthworks. A rectangular stockade and other enclosures had associated ox burials, and ritual pits containing animal burials including pig bones and skulls. A pig's head, cut in half, lay on the body of a man buried with a chariot at Garton. Numerous chalk figurines have been found: miniature warriors with sword at belt and every head snapped off – a reminder of the ritual killing of objects and the Celtic cult of the severed head.

At Garton Slack a youth and a woman of around thirty had been buried pinned together, and to the ground, by a wooden stake. The controversial interpretation of the excavator, Tony Brewster, was that they were buried alive in a punitive or ritual killing, a premature baby being expelled during the woman's death throes. At Wetwang three chariot burials were discovered in a line. The large central mound contained the rich burial of a woman; in the two smaller mounds warriors were buried with identical swords.

Below: A lorry raises chalk dust on its way to the quarry face (the dark triangle at the centre of the photograph) in the valley below Wetwang Grange.

Wookey Hole Caves, Wells, Somerset

A spectacular cave system hollowed out by the River Axe on its journey to the Bristol Channel from high on the Mendips. Twenty-five chambers and caverns linked by a plunging, tortuous channel have been explored by divers. Four caverns are accessible to the public, the vast walls glittering with stalactites set against the deep red of iron oxide. The caves were occupied in the Iron Age and Roman period, one chamber being used as a family burial place. The remains of at least twenty-eight individuals were found in the chamber, along with pots, jewellery and other artefacts. In the Witch's Kitchen broods a sinister stalagmite staring at the underground water. In profile, the formation has the sunken mouth and pointed chin of the child-eating witch, turned to stone with a splash of holy water by an exorcizing monk. Pottery and human remains, especially skulls, found near the witch suggest ritual use, but they were probably carried downstream from the burial chamber. Steps just visible on the left of the witch were cut down to the river in the Iron Age. The subterranean system and river presided over by a huge head must have held a deep fascination for the inhabitants of the caves.

Dung and skeletons, a pot and the charred stump of a tethering post found in the outer cave suggest it was used to stable and milk goats. In a rock fissure nearby lay a fully clothed skeleton equipped with a dagger, knife, bill-hook and alabaster ball – an unfortunate peasant overcome by smoke, or the black witch of Welsh legend 'who lived in a cave at the head of the Stream of Sorrow on the confines of Hell' and was slain by King Arthur.

Uffington White Horse, Wantage, Oxfordshire

Resembling the dragon-like horses on Belgic coins, the Uffington White Horse has been described as a tribal emblem and cult animal representing the Celtic goddess Epona. Others have seen it as Saxon, connected with Hengist, or with myths of the god Woden (Odin), or a celebration of Alfred's victory against the Norse in 871 AD at the battle of Ashdown. Recent excavations by the Oxford Archaeological Unit have pierced some of the figure's mysteries. The image was

constructed by digging trenches into the brown hill-wash deposits and packing them with chalk. Despite recutting and the traditional 'scouring' every seven years, the cartoon shape is largely original: the body has become a little thinner, the beak shorter. Dowser Guy Underwood (1974) believed the horse was based on lines of force created by underground water, the eye marking a 'blind spring' from which streams radiate. The horse stares at Uffington Castle to the south-west, a hillfort begun in the seventh century BC. Between them, close to the horse, sit the remains of a Neolithic long mound – used again in the Roman period for cremations and inhumations, including bodies decapitated after death – and a

Bronze Age round barrow reused for Saxon burials. Roman coins and other material scattered inside the fort may reflect its later use as a fairground or shrine site. A massive post-hole at the highest point of the interior conjures the torc-wearing timber images of continental sacred enclosures. Optical dating, a new technique indicating when buried soil was last exposed to sunlight, suggests that the horse trenches were dug in the Late Bronze Age, around 3,000 years ago: that is, after the barrows but before the fort. Whatever the true date, the figure is typical of Celtic iconography – powerful, vigorous, stylized, abstract – representing essence and ideal, in recognizable short-hand, rather than everyday reality.

Above: A *view from the north-west with the hillfort on the right.*

Inset: *Looking northwards over eye and beak to the flat-topped mound of Dragon Hill, where Christian legend places St George slaying the worm of paganism.*

Cerne Giant, Cerne Abbas, Dorset

For obvious reasons, this naked giant is considered to be a fertility god – probably a pre-Roman Celtic 'father of the gods and ancestor of the people', such as the club-wielding Dagdá of Irish legends, or Cernunnos, sometimes depicted as a giant with a club. A second-century-AD cult figure of the Roman emperor Commodus as Hercules has also been suggested. In medieval documents the giant is god to the heathen Saxons, a 'preserver of health' variously called Heil, Hegle, Helis or Helith – names with ancient elements denoting

the sun, health and holy. By tradition the chalk was scoured every seventh year (it was done in April 1995 by National Trust volunteers), the well-being of local herds and fields depending on preservation of the image. Until the last century a maypole was erected on the mound inside the Frying Pan or Trendle – the earthwork enclosure above the giant's head – for dances, revels, fertility rites and generally uninhibited behaviour around May Day and midsummer each year. Young women on their wedding eve would walk around, or sleep on, the giant to ensure a happy, fruitful marriage. Couples seeking children would make petitions and offerings at the 'wishing well' in the village before ascending the hill to the giant and the enclosure. A resistivity survey carried out by Rodney Castleden has located patterns of

disturbance in the soil, suggesting that the giant once had a cloak over his left shoulder and a severed head at his left hand, making him resemble naked warriors seen on Iron Age coins. It seems that when the penis was recut, after being masked by scrub in Victorian times, it was lengthened by incorporating the originally separate navel. A dowsing survey convinced Guy Underwood that the figure traced force lines caused by underground water, and the low mound by the left hand was an obliterated second phallus, identifying the god as Cronus who castrated his father Uranus. Ronald Hutton has argued the giant is a seventeenth-century folly, with the earliest authentic reference to the figure dating from 1694.

St Augustine's Well, Cerne Abbas, Dorset

Strange stories were told in the eleventh and twelfth centuries of St Augustine coming as a missionary to the hamlet of 'Cernel' around AD 600. After rejection by the local people, who pelted him with mud and tied cows' tails to his coat, he walked up the valley, washed himself in this spring and, looking skywards, 'saw God' – the giant? Other details include him cursing the villagers' children to be born with tails. When this began to come true, he was able to return, convert the people and baptize them in the newly blessed well. He withdrew the curse, broke in pieces their pagan idol Heil and founded the abbey in celebration. Local belief persists that the descendants of those cursed by the saint have elongated tail bones. Wishes and offerings are still made at the well, which, along with the giant, retains its ancient association with fertility.

Swastika Stone, Ilkley, West Yorkshire

The carving is based on nine hollows or 'cups' making a five by five cross. A groove winds in and out of the cups to form four curving anticlockwise arms, one of which has attached to it a reversed question mark with a cup at its centre. The sophistication and similarity to Celtic art symbols, such as the wind-play motif, makes the design later than the Bronze Age cup-and-ring carvings found on the surrounding moors. The form is identical to 'Celtic rose' designs at Carpene di Sellero (Italy), dated to 800–700 BC. The curved arms and basic cross make the Ilkley swastika different from the traditional, angular nine-pointed emblem of luck, good fortune and well-being seen in Hindu ritual, on objects from Troy and Mycenae, on axe models from Switzerland, in Roman mosaics such as that at Lullingstone villa (Kent) and as reversed by the Nazis. Ancient use of the swastika made it symbolize the sky and the movement of the sun, while the wheel represented the sun itself. The outcrop on Woodhouse Crag overlooks the Wharfe valley and Ilkley, where the parish church stands on the site of a Roman fort. Celtic stone heads have been found in the area, and an altar dedicated to Verbeia, goddess of the River Wharfe.

Casterley Camp, Upavon, Wiltshire

The earthworks look like a hillfort, but are in a weak defensive position overlooked from the west, astride a spur and with three simple entrances. The single ditch and bank rampart does not make best use of the slopes and was not completed. The northern projection in the photograph may have been a late change of plan to create a stronger line of defence. Near the centre was a series of square and oval areas defined by ditches and banks now destroyed by ploughing. In the oval enclosure a massive post stood in a large pit, with four human skeletons and fourteen red deer antlers arranged around it. These features are older than the rampart, which may have been added to protect or enhance an important religious sanctuary centred on ancestor burials or sacrifices.

Hayling Island, Hampshire

Dark marks tracing out a circle and rectangles in a growing crop revealed the site of an Iron Age shrine and Roman temple. The first-century-BC shrine resembled a domestic round house with a shallow-porched entrance on the east and a large pit at the centre. The shrine sat within a squarish enclosure defined by a fence and hedge, with a ditch beyond. A three-sided square of fencing within the enclosure partly screened the shrine entrance. Cult activity occurred in the open, with votives placed in the ditch and courtyard. Ritually damaged horse and chariot trappings, pieces of scabbard, spearheads, sword-shaped currency bars, brooches and 170 Celtic coins were deposited, along with meat offerings of pig and sheep, and pots containing food and drink. Soon after the Roman conquest, the shrine was replaced by a substantial stone tower of similar but slightly larger plan. The enclosure became a larger rectangular temple precinct or temenos, similar to a free-standing monastic cloister. The limestone tower was plastered a red colour on the outside and was multicoloured on the inside. It had a porched entrance on the east, facing the entrance hall in the precinct wall.

The tower cella is of a type better known in France, such as at Périgueux. It may have been built by Gaulish masons for the client king Cogidumnus, who also had a villa-style palace at nearby Fishbourne, just west of Chichester. He was set up by the Romans to rule over the local pro-Roman tribes. Here we have a Celtic king, possibly brought from Gaul, converting a native shrine, sacred perhaps to warriors and the war god Teutates, into a Gallo-Roman temple of Mars.

CHAPTER TWO

ROMANO -CELTIC BRITAIN

ONQUERING new territories was the usual answer to the problems of Rome. Julius Caesar led campaigns against southern England in 55 and 54 BC. Although the campaigns were inconclusive, he won several battles, weakening hostile tribes while strengthening contacts with friendly ones. In AD 40 Caligula assembled troops to cross the Channel but, unsure of their discipline, or just plain mad, he ordered them to fill helmets with shells, which were then sent to Rome as spoils of war against the sea. In 43 Aulus Plautius, general of Emperor Claudius, had similar trouble making his troops embark for a country beyond the known world. A pep talk from the imperial freedman Narcissus finally shamed and humoured them into action. Claudius needed to win respect for himself and his discredited imperial family. New income was urgently required after Caligula's excesses and, following the death of Cunobelinus, the British princes' political upheavals were threatening Roman interests in southern England and Gaul. Plautius subdued the tribes around Kent and Essex, allowing Claudius himself to lead the army into Cunobelinus's former stronghold to receive the submission of 'eleven British kings'. Forts and towns were founded, existing routes incorporated into a system of military roads, civilians banned from carrying weapons and rich villas built on country estates; life became rigidly structured, controlled and urbanized. Roman gods were introduced, equated with local deities and a plethora of hybrids were worshipped. 'Naturalistic' religious figures of stone and alloy were used, along with stone altars and inscriptions.

A compromise between Celtic and classical tastes evolved in the form of Romano-Celtic temples, many built on the sites of earlier shrines. Offerings were still made to natural features; sacred shafts were dug and ritually filled, their contents reflecting increasing 'consumerism' and a sense of individual importance. Healing cults to gods such as Nodens (Celtic), Apollo (Roman) and Sulis Minerva (hybrid) flourished at Lydney (Forest of Dean), Nettleton Shrub (Wiltshire) and Bath (Somerset). At Lydney and Pagans Hill (Somerset), dormitories, or abatons, were built for incubation, sacred sleep bringing cures and prophetic dreams. People from all over the empire came into Britain, creating an exotic mix of cultures and beliefs in even the most remote military outposts. New religions included the rival Eastern mystery cults of Mithraism and Christianity. Persecution of Christians had much to do with their refusing to take an oath of loyalty to the emperor as head of the official imperial cult. Acknowledging only one god was a matter of principle for the Christians, but to Romans, normally tolerant of and pragmatic about other gods, refusing to participate in the state religion was treason. Initially Mithraism thrived while Christianity continued a small, secretive and rebellious sect. In a dramatic reversal of policy, the persecutions ended in 311, Christianity becoming the religion of the empire under Constantine. The Edict of Milan in 313 confirmed the peace of the Church and in 314 British bishops attended the Council of Arles. Theodosius made sacrifices illegal, closed pagan temples to the public and banned domestic worship of the household guardians; no incense was to be burned or garlands displayed.

At the same time as Christianity was being accepted, the Roman hold on Britain was being weakened by political struggles inside the empire and by new and numerous barbarian threats from outside. The west coast of Britain was prey to Irish raiders, Picts swarmed over Hadrian's Wall, while Germanic peoples pressed against the forts of the eastern 'Saxon Shore'. As Alaric and his Goths advanced to sack Rome itself in 410, the Romano-British were abandoned to their fate.

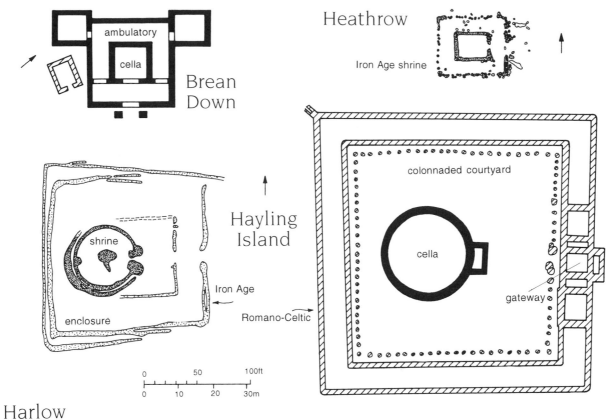

ambulatory

cella

Brean
Down

Heathrow

Iron Age shrine

colonnaded courtyard

cella

gateway

Hayling
Island

shrine

Iron Age

enclosure

Romano-Celtic

0   50   100ft

0   10   20   30m

SCHEMATIC PLANS OF
IRON-AGE SHRINES AND
ROMANO-CELTIC TEMPLES

Harlow

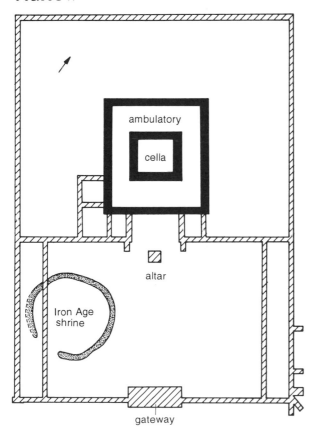

ambulatory

cella

altar

Iron Age
shrine

gateway

Gosbecks

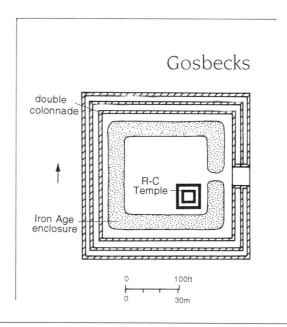

double
colonnade

R-C
Temple

Iron Age
enclosure

0   100ft

0   30m

Gosbecks Archaeological Park, Colchester, Essex

Gosbecks was the royal farmstead and religious enclosure at the heart of Camulodunum – fortress of the war god, Camulos – stronghold of Cunobelin, King of the Catuvellauni. The town of Colchester grew from the Roman fort established 2 miles to the north-east of Camulodunum's defensive earthworks. The deep ditch of the Iron Age enclosure retains moisture showing as a dark band against the surrounding parched grass. Around AD 100 a small, square Romano-Celtic temple was built in the south-east corner of the enclosure and the still open ditch surrounded by a concentric walled and colonnaded portico (marked by white lines in the photograph), with an eastern entrance matching the causeway across the ditch.

The whole complex sat within a walled enclosure 1,000 feet long, just outside the northern end of which a bronze statuette of Mercury, the god of trade, was ploughed up in 1945. The inner temple, which was reserved for priests and the privileged few, had a tall, roofed central cella surrounded by an open colonnaded area. Outside this, within the ditched enclosure, stood altars and shrines to several Roman gods. At festivals large numbers of people were able to stand in the outer colonnade watching ceremonies taking place in the temple and enclosure across the open ditch. A 'D'-shaped theatre built at the same time just to the south, seating 4,000–5,000 people, was also used for religious ceremonies, as well as dramatic performances, speeches and assemblies.

Harlow Temple, Essex

A Romano-Celtic temple was built in the first century AD on the summit of a long, thin, low hill enclosed by an Iron Age earthwork. The temple initially comprised a square cella and ambulatory within a palisade. Later a walled and terraced precinct was built around the temple. An ornamental gateway at the south-east led into the lower courtyard, where an altar stood at the bottom of steps leading up to the entrance porch of the temple. A large, helmeted limestone head from the cult figure of Minerva was found in the rubble, along with a roughly carved Roman warrior-god. A lead 'curse' tablet was also found: 'To the god Mercury, I entrust to you my affair with Eterna and her own self, and may Timotheus feel no jealousy of me at risk of his life-blood.' The temple was dismantled and robbed in the late fourth century, possibly by local Roman Christians. The lower courtyard had been built over an Iron Age shrine in the form of a round house with an entrance at the south. Over 800 Celtic coins, mostly bronze but some gold and silver, were found in pre-Roman levels in or near the shrine. Many were in mint condition; they may have been buried or suspended in some way inside the shrine. Other finds included jewellery, especially brooches; iron tools, including plough-shares; numerous metal strips and many lamb and other bones – the remains of offerings and feasts. After excavation the site was landscaped and marked out in concrete slabs and blocks. The replica, standing in an open area of grass and scrub amid factories south of the River Stort, has itself become a ruin – littered, overgrown and vandalized.

Woodeaton,
Islip, Oxfordshire

The broad, double-doored gateway to the temenos (sacred precinct) at Woodeaton faced eastwards, towards the dawn. A religious complex was built here early in the Roman period, just north of a native settlement, on a site which may have been an Iron Age sacred enclosure. Erected on stone supports, the first temple had a half-timbered super-structure with plastered walls and a tiled roof. Rebuilt on a grander scale in the second century AD, the open colonnade of the ambulatory may have been replaced by a solid wall (with small windows) to keep out the chill winds of this exposed hillside. The wall of the rectangular central cella could have been solid, with rounded arches giving access from the surrounding corridors, or made of columns, allowing a continuous view of the inner sanctum. The whole building could have been covered by a four-sided sloping roof, but it is more likely that the cella rose at least one storey above the lean-to roofs of the 'reversed cloisters' of the ambulatory corridors. Lighting the central space, windows in the upper part of the cella also allowed smoke from lamps, sacred fires and offerings to escape; several levels of a central hearth were found. The temple did not stand in the middle of the temenos and the gateway was not centrally placed in the eastern wall. This arrangement, noted at other sites, may mean the centre was left symbolically empty or something important but perishable formed the heart of the sanctuary – a wicker structure, timber image or animal head and skin propped up like a tent on poles.

No sign of other buildings or permanent occupation was found within the temenos, which is best described as a periodic fairground with flourishing commercial activity connected with practice of the cult. The distribution of finds around the gateway suggests rows of stalls and booths selling secular goods, votive objects, such as miniature bronze spears and axes, and keepsakes much as can be found at major pilgrim sites today. One has to imagine the hurly-burly of a fair and a market, mixed with the piety and fervour of a religious festival. Bracelets, rings and over 1,100 coins came from around the entrance pathway – another common feature of such sites – indicating a religious act involving the 'offering' of tokens on arrival at a sacred site or while approaching its ritual focus. Representations of Venus, Cupid, Minerva and Mars were found, with examples of Jupiter's eagle, a trident-shaped object, and ritually bent model spears completing the symbols of 'love' and 'war'. Other items suggest cults of healing and female fecundity: bronze snakes may have been used as childbirth charms. Letters of bronze spelled the names of gods and supplicants. Use of the religious complex may have continued after the Roman period; certainly a Saxon charter refers to a 'coloured floor' at Woodeaton.

Farley Heath, Albury, Surrey

The site of a Romano-Celtic temple and walled polygonal temenos after excavation and topsoil replacement in summer 1995. Opposing corners of the inner and outer squares of the temple are marked by concrete. The central cella may have been a solid-walled tower, with an entrance and windows, surrounded by four verandas with columns. Robbed of stone in the seventeenth century, disastrously 'excavated' in the 1840s, the temple was worked on again early this century. Illegal metal-detecting in the 1990s caused further damage, destroying what little remained of the archaeological stratigraphy. Over 200 holes had been dug by treasure-hunters in search of goodies, the details and archaeological contexts of which went unrecorded because they were stolen from a scheduled ancient monument. The excavation by Surrey County Council was to clear the site of finds and salvage any archaeological details from the sorry mess. The temple was built in a remote and rural location in the border area between two Celtic tribes, the Atrebates and the Regni. A Roman spur road ran N–S, just west of the temple, joining two main roads running south-west and west-south-west from London. Built in the first century AD, the complex may have replaced an Iron Age site and was in use into the 400s. Rural temples took over many of the ceremonial, trading, administrative, judicial and social functions of the earlier shrines and hillforts. That the temple complex was of very special social and religious importance is suggested by the spur road and the unusual nature of the finds. Stone, flint and bronze tools of the Neolithic and Bronze Age were found, including stone axes representing thunderbolts in the worship of sky gods Jupiter and Taranis. Other finds included an enamelled stand or miniature stool, sea urchins, glass beads, brooches, barbed and tanged arrowheads and at least 70 Iron Age coins, and

over 1,000 more were said to have come from the temenos in the 1840s. The recording of these finds was so poor, however, that it is impossible to tell if they were deposited individually, scattered by the handful or the result of periodic cleaning out of votive deposits from inside the cella. The most significant finds were a priest's crown – consisting of three pieces of chain attached to a central knobbed bronze disc – and sceptre binding. The sheet-bronze binding was decorated with stylized figures of animals and 'gods', perhaps Jupiter and Vulcan, with symbolic objects including a solar wheel and tongs. Reports of Roman tiles and masonry at Skemp Pond, 100 yards to the south-east, had led to suggestions that the spring-fed hollow was the original sacred site, but excavations in autumn 1995 were unable to confirm this.

Maiden Castle, Dorset

Three lines of massive ramparts, with complicated entrances at each end, defend the two knolls and shallow saddle of an E–W ridge. The initial eastern compound of the hillfort, built on the site of a Neolithic causewayed camp, contained several shrines and temples in use at various times from the early Iron Age through to the post-Roman period. The fort was stormed by Vespasian's troops around AD 45, leaving the inhabitants to bury their dead outside the east gate in shallow graves cut through a layer of ashes. By 60 the whole population of the fort had moved down to the Roman town of Dorchester. Around 350 – when Christianity was the official Roman religion – a circular pagan temple was built, in stone, within the foundations of an Iron Age timber shrine. A little later a Romano-Celtic temple was built just to the north-east. A tiny two-roomed structure nearby has been interpreted as the pagan priest's house or a later Christian chapel. There was a strong reaction in rural districts against the rapid rise of Christianity in towns, and among the aristocracy and moneyed classes (the term pagan comes from the Latin *paganus*, meaning a country dweller or rustic peasant). central shrine is surrounded by an ambulatory, both with doorways facing south-east down a pathway to the fort's eastern entrance. An infant foundation burial was found between the inner and outer walls on the north-east (rear right in the photograph). The ramparts of the eastern enclosure were refurbished to create a temenos and stone gateway for the temples. One hundred and seventy-one coins dated to 350–60 came from the circular temple. From the Romano-Celtic temple came a plaque of Minerva, a nude female figurine and a silvered bronze triple-horned bull with (originally) three female figures on its back: a myth or cult image, illustrating shape-shifting or the multiple aspects of a deity.

Muntham Court, West Sussex

A circular hut on this hillside, near the break of slope, was used as a shrine. Three ox skulls had been placed on top of bones buried in pits beneath the hut floor, which was covered in pottery shards and votive bronze objects. A baked clay model of a human leg was also found. A low mound in front of the hut contained a mass of Roman pottery, with more bronze and iron objects, including ceremonial knives, part of a saw, a fish-shaped enamelled brooch and a small plaque of a 'dying' boar. The mound may have been constructed to receive offerings or formed from ritual debris cleared out of the shrine. It covered an area of Iron Age post-holes, pottery and pot boilers – fire-heated stones placed in water for cooking, or scattered with water to create steam for saunas or sacred sweat lodges. A Roman well at the bottom of the hill contained pottery and many skeletons of dogs – animals connected with healing and the underworld. Copies of Roman pottery and Romano-Celtic shrines and temples were in use at Lancing Ring and Slonk Hill to the south-east. To the north-east, visible in the photograph as a lone clump of beeches, is Chactonbury Ring, a small hillfort with a later temple.

Chanctonbury Ring, Washington, West Sussex

An octagonal temple had attached on its east a rectangular structure containing numerous pigs' teeth and jawbones. As at Muntham Court, cattle skulls and depictions of boars were also found. Pork was the main feasting meat of the Celts; the choicest joints were the right of champions – the 'hero's portion'. Frequent finds of boar plaques and brooches from the South Downs suggest a cult among the local tribes. The boar – a ferocious animal – was often chosen as a clan totem; with bristles raised it formed a suitable battle amulet or standard.

Jordan Hill, Weymouth, Dorset

Stone foundations to the central shrine of a Romano-Celtic temple overlooking Weymouth Bay. A pavement and portico encircling the cella were located, but the outer wall was not: the design may have been unusual or the masonry completely robbed out and the trenches then not recognized in the excavations of 1843 and 1931–2. The temple faced towards the east within a square temenos enclosing the hilltop near a Roman cemetery. A dry well in the far (south-east) corner was lined with clay and tiles set on edge. A stone cist had been constructed on a bed of clay at the bottom of the shaft. Within it were placed two Roman urns, an iron sword, spearhead and knife, two iron bars and a steelyard. Above this was a thick layer of tiles, then ashes. Above this, a sandwich of two tiles with a filling of a bird skeleton and coin was repeated sixteen times. This was interrupted half-way up by another cist of stones with two urns and an iron sword and spearhead. The species – presumably carefully chosen for cult purposes – were crow, raven, buzzard and starling. Bird bones have been found in Roman shafts at Ewell (Surrey), Newstead (Borders) and at Northfleet (Kent). At Hockwold (Norfolk) pig and bird bones were buried under the four birch-column bases of the temple cella. In several of the temples at Springhead (Kent) bird bones were deposited, including a headless foundation burial along with four human infants, two of which had also been decapitated.

Brean Down, Weston Bay, Somerset

The dramatic headland of hard limestone in the Bristol Channel was an island until medieval drainage work created a narrow neck of marshy pasture. Bronze Age round barrows, an Iron Age promontory fort and embanked field systems survive on the raised land, with a Bronze Age settlement and early Christian cemetery at the cliff base. A late Roman temple – another example of rural paganism in Christian times – was built directly on to the rock just north of the most obvious barrow. Made of limestone, it had a square cella surrounded by a three-sided ambulatory, with a vestibule across the full width of the front. A porch was added to the entrance on the south-east, and two square annexes were attached to the rear-side corners. Later a small rectangular drystone building was erected to the south using material robbed from the temple. Its single room contained a hearth and the domestic items of a 'squatter' or religious hermit. Finds from the temple included a bronze leaf, spoon, bracelet and ring, an iron stylus, bone pins and nearly 500 coins.

Bar Hill, Twechar, Strathclyde

Bar Hill fort is one of a series strung along the Antonine Wall, the turf-built frontier defence between the Clyde and Forth estuaries, completed around AD 142 to accompany a temporary Roman advance. A well in the courtyard of the headquarters building had been deliberately filled. The main items were a wooden bucket and pulley wheel, large pieces of oak, bones of cattle and sheep, deer antlers, oyster shells, hazelnuts and hawthorn twigs, arrowheads, leather boots, coins, iron objects and tools placed inside a bag inside a large amphora, two inscriptions, and column-shafts with their capitals and bases. Some of the objects are of the sort found in votive shafts; others could be from\ dismantling or destruction around the final withdrawal of the garrison in the 160s. Anne Ross (Ross and Cyprien 1985) suggests the well was used by the Damnonii, before and after the Roman occupation, as a ritual focus for a sacred precinct or grove. Bar Hill is a possible location for the Celtic sanctuary of Medionemeton listed in the *Ravenna Cosmography*.

Newstead Roman Fort, Melrose, Borders

Agricola founded a major fort and supply depot on the south bank of the Tweed around AD 81. Commanding the ford and vital N–S route, for 100 years it was the communication centre and heart of the Roman occupation network of southern Scotland. Named Trimontium after the three-peaked Eildon Hills to the south-west, it neutralized the hillfort capital of the Selgovae on the northern summit containing over 300 huts. The Romans used the hilltop to site a wooden signal tower capable of sending and receiving messages from up to 20 miles away. The flat ground occupied by the Roman fort between hill and river may have been used before the conquest as a Celtic sacred precinct.

Over 100 pits and shafts contained a mass of objects open to various interpretations: metal tools, utensils and weapons including armour and helmets; coins and jewellery; stone altars and a horse figurine; human skulls and complete skeletons; shoes and pieces of leather, basketwork, whole pots and shards; wheels; many animal bones including whole horses and dogs, and numerous horse, dog and cattle skulls; many deer antlers; oak branches, twigs, a steering oar and plank; birch twigs and a 9-foot branch; oyster shells and hazelnuts. Some may be seen as rubbish pits, others as stashes or dumps of surplus equipment buried when the Romans had to abandon the fort. Some are pre-Roman, used for votive and ritual purposes, which probably continued during the life of the fort. The contents of a pit lined with red sandstone blocks included an altar to Jupiter, a complete human skeleton and two skulls, iron tools, armour and coins, cattle bones, deer antlers and numerous horse skulls. One pit had only a human skeleton standing upright on the bottom; another contained nine complete horses, one human female adult buried with a dog skull, a cow skull, pottery-shards, oyster shells and hazelnuts, and an iron hammer, stylus, ring and saw. The quantity of horse remains, especially skulls and whole skeletons, suggests cult use.

Above: *Trimontium fort memorial with Eildon Hill North beyond.*

Right: *Looking north-east from Eildon Hill North hillfort. The Roman fort is in the large central field divided by a hedge with trees.*

Nettleton Shrub, Castle Combe, Wiltshire

This lane follows the course of the Bath–Cirencester section of the Fosse Way, a Roman frontier road. Soon after AD 69 a small circular shrine had been built on a Celtic cult site beside the Broadmead Brook. By the third century a thriving religious complex had filled the area west (right) of the road, between the stream and hilltop. The simple shrine had become an octagonal temple with a central circular cella surrounded by eight chambers and a colonnaded walkway. The range of buildings indicated industrial and domestic use, along with accommodation and facilities for resident priests and numerous visiting pilgrims. Mercury was worshipped, but inscriptions and offerings show the primary function was a healing sanctuary presided over by Apollo the archer. An altar styles him 'Cunomaglos', the 'Hound Lord' in charge of the chase and sacred dogs with healing saliva.

In the fourth century four of the temple chambers were sealed up, leaving a Maltese cross with a circular centre. This may reflect Christian use, but similar blocking off, creating 'secret' rooms, took place at other temple sites where pagan worship continued. The final use was Christian, possibly even monastic. The buildings were set on fire at least twice by Irish pirates raiding via the Bristol Channel. In the early fifth century things came to a violent end, as revealed by the sword-slashed bones and decapitated skeletons of the final inhabitants.

Below: *The Normans built the King's Bath over the ruined reservoir, which had been constructed around an ancient thermal spring.*

Roman Baths Museum, Bath, Somerset

The King's Bath

Towards the end of the first century AD a healing sanctuary was built around a thermal spring sacred to the Celtic goddess Sulis, whom the Romans equated with Minerva. The sanctuary had high status and was widely known. Influential people came from all over the Roman world to dedicate altars and make offerings of Celtic silver coins to the spring from a causeway of boulders and gravel across the steaming mud. The Romans built a large, lead-lined reservoir around the spring as the focus of the new complex. The King's Bath was built by the Normans over the ruined reservoir; the spring still bubbles up through tons of collapsed Roman masonry deep underneath the bath floor. Even when the reservoir was later enclosed in a building, it was possible to look from the baths, over the spring, to the main sacrificial altar standing in the paved courtyard before the east front of the temple. The temple, of true classical design, stood on a high podium. Steps led up to a porch with four fluted Corinthian columns topped by a pediment.

Temple pediment

At the centre of the pediment a circular shield with baleful head was held aloft by two winged Victories, accompanied in the corners by two tritons with Minerva's attributes of helmet and owl below. As indication of her martial prowess, Minerva often had on her shield, or breastplate, a petrifying Medusa head with hissing serpents for hair. In this case the Gorgon has a male 'Celtic' face with beard, moustache and penetrating gaze. With hair that could also be flames or water, he resembles representations of the sun, and the classical sea gods Oceanus or Neptune. In one enigmatic image the Celtic-Roman fusion of Sulis Minerva worshipped at Bath has been symbolized. Within the temple cella stood a classical cult statue of Minerva: the life-sized gilded bronze head can be seen in the museum. It is possible that the healing complex was designed as a monument to reconciliation between Romans and native Celts, when the horrors of and recriminations following Boudicca's rebellion of AD 60 had begun to fade.

Overflow drain

The emerging water is believed to be several thousand years old. Rain falling on the Mendip Hills slowly sank into the limestone, to be heated deep in the earth before rising again, travelling along fissures and faults to burst free at Bath. The flow is 13 litres per second, *c.* 250,000 gallons a day, at 115 °F. The water contains forty-three minerals, with a high iron content which causes the orange staining. It may be sampled – along with more substantial nourishment – to the accompaniment of classical musicians in the the elegant surroundings of the Pump Room. The spring rose in the reservoir, which acted as a settling tank, creating a head of water distributed in lead pipes around the baths and fountains. Sediment was washed from the reservoir via a large overflow drain, the arch of which was designed to impress.

The Great Bath

Steps on all sides descend to a flat bottom lined with forty-five sheets of Mendip lead. Originally there was a vaulted roof rather than the open arrangement of Victorian restoration. The baths included warm and hot rooms with bathing pools, a very hot, dry sauna and a cold plunge to close the pores after bathing, massaging with perfumed oil and scraping clean with a strigil. Mixed bathing was stopped in the second century by order of Emperor Hadrian. Activities included sports, debating and gossiping, listening to philosophical discourses and entertaining clients – 'I'm sorry, Severinus is at the baths just now. May I take a message?' Bath was an exhibition of Roman middle-class concerns: healing and recreation, trade and commerce, offerings and dedications, and jealousy and revenge. Along with ritually damaged coins, the usual trinkets and votive pleas for healing, including carved ivory breasts, over 100 *defixiones* or curse tablets have been recovered from the sacred spring: handwritten messages on sheets of lead or pewter requesting punishment of a rival, enemy, unknown thief or list of suspects. In legal formulas, often with words written backwards, spiteful and vicious requests were made against the vital organs and processes of the accused. A goddess who could heal could also harm.

Minerva Shrine, Chester, Cheshire

Minerva was also worshipped at Chester, where a shrine was carved on a first-century-AD quarry-face. Sandstone outcrops on the south bank of the River Dee, beside the Roman road and ford, were a source of building materials for the legionary fortress. The much-weathered figure is identified as Minerva by her owl of wisdom, and helmet, spear and shield of war. She was probably invoked here in her role as patron of craftsmanship and the arts. Offerings were placed on top of the carved altar at the base of the column on the left. Some believe the carving is of Deva, the Celtic goddess of the river Dee, after whom the Romans named their fort. Modern offerings of flowers are made to the image and coins are hidden in the cracks.

Lady's Well, Holystone, Northumberland

This holy well is on the course of the Roman branch road running SW–NE between Dere Street (A68), and the Devil's Causeway (A697), the main roads running

north-west and north-east from Corbridge by Hadrian's Wall. The stone-lined pool and walled enclosure may originally date from Roman or medieval times; repair work was undertaken and a cross and statue were added in the eighteenth and nineteenth centuries. St Ninian in the fifth century and St Paulinus in the seventh are reputed to have used the well to baptize Christian converts.

The name Lady's Well came into use after a priory of Augustinian canonesses dedicated to St Mary the Virgin was established in the twelfth century. The original lady may have been a Celtic goddess presiding over a healing spring that was adopted by the Romans and subsequently taken over by wandering Christian missionaries travelling the Roman roads.

Shrine to Cocidius, Yardhope

Roman soldiers going to the fort of Bremenium (High Rochester) on Dere Street in Redesdale, 9 miles away, must have been glad of the spring. They built a marching camp at Yardhope on the road 2 miles south-west of Lady's Well. Near to the camp – but on MoD land and not accessible – is a tiny cell built among rocks looking eastwards. It has a carved bench-bed, a hearth and flue, a chiselled groove to support a sloping roof, and the hole of a post which held the door. Too small for even one person to live in, the rock chamber may have been a shrine to the god of the place. An image and shelf, possibly for a lamp and offerings, are cut in the rock face just outside the doorway. The naked figure, holding a spear and shield, is Celtic in style but carved by someone with Roman training. The most likely Celtic warrior god from around Hadrian's Wall is Cocidius, the 'Red One', equated by the Romans with Mars. A native shrine may have been utilized by Roman soldiers feeling in need of martial aid, seeking to appease the god of a hostile area. It seems appropriate that a possible refuge for Roman soldiers should have been used as a bivouac by modern soldiers on manoeuvres on the Otterburn Training Range.

Coventina's Well, Carrawburgh, Northumberland

This marshy ground, west of the Roman fort of Brocolitia at Carrawburgh, was sacred to Coventina, a Celtic spring-goddess. When Roman engineers were constructing the ditch and banks of the *vallum* running behind Hadrian's Wall, they built a square cistern here to control the spring and drain the marsh. By AD 133 the fort had been built over the *vallum* and the well enclosed within a stone wall. With the well as a cella, the outer wall formed the double-square plan of a Romano-Celtic temple, but with the entrance on the west, facing away from the fort. Coventina was probably a local native goddess concerned with healing who was worshipped as a water nymph. Her cult reached its peak around the early third century, when soldiers with Celtic

superstitions, in need of a mother and a goddess, regularly asked for her aid and protection. The well was carefully sealed and hidden in the fourth century, as if to keep it from harm. Over 1,300 coins came from the well; some 300 of brass, commemorating the defeat of the Brigantes by Antoninus Pius, show Britannia with her head bowed. Altars were dedicated to Coventina in her single and triple forms. Some of the altars bore suspension rings, suggesting that they were dipped into the water to give and receive blessings. Other finds included pins and brooches, bronze figurines of a horse and dog, decorative copper alloy heads from buckets or cauldrons, part of a human skull, pottery and glass, shrine bells and a baked clay incense burner.

Temple of Mithras, Carrawburgh, Northumberland

Christianity's great rival was Mithraism, another Eastern mystery-religion in which a deity (Mithras) depicted as the power of light (good) waged constant battle against the power of darkness (evil). It too demanded high standards of conduct and promised salvation and joy in the world to come. The Magi visiting the infant Jesus were astrologers of the Persian court, priests of the cult of Mithras. Its exclusively male followers achieved membership of seven ascending grades of initiation via rigorous ordeals of fire, water and fasting. This temple was built around AD 200, damaged c. 297, extensively refurbished, then desecrated and used as a rubbish tip in the fourth century, when Christianity was becoming the official Roman religion. Near the entrance on the left stood a ceremonial hearth and pit used in initiation ordeals, some of which involved a bull being slaughtered over an initiate lying blood-soaked in a trench. A statuette of a mother goddess (probably Coventina) stood in the ante-chapel, screened off from the nave. Worshippers sat on raised benches in the darkened aisles. The nave contained four tiny altars and figures of Cautes and Cautopates, the torch bearing helpers of Mithras: east and west, dawn and twilight. Three altars stood at the far end, with a shelf behind supporting the dramatically lit bull-slaying relief.

Mithras was sent to earth to restore light out of darkness and evil, and to tame wild elements of creation by liberating the blood of growth and regeneration. The temples were designed to represent a sacred cave, itself a representation of the universe, where the mystery began. The original sculptures and a reconstruction of the temple can be seen in the Museum of Antiquities at Newcastle University. The ground plan of another such temple, the Walbrook Mithraeum, is laid out in Temple Court, 11 Queen Victoria Street, London EC4.

Benwell Roman Temple, Newcastle upon Tyne, Tyne and Wear

Near the fort of Condercum on Hadrian's Wall, a small Roman temple with an apse contained altars dedicated to a local native god, Antenociticus (Anociticus). One of the altars was erected by a cavalry officer from the fort celebrating his promotion to *quaestor'* a lucrative combination of tax collector and military paymaster. The stone cult head shows a classical youth with a Celtic look in his eyes, and grooved hair. The head, with faint signs of a torc around the neck, may have been broken from a larger statue.

Right: *The southern defences of the Roman town. The medieval church stands at its centre, adjacent to the site of the forum.*

Caerwent, Gwent

A Roman regional capital and 'market town' of the hostile but subdued Silures. Some of the town's wells were used for cult purposes. A statuette of a seated mother goddess was placed in one, along with a collection of iron tools. Another held five dog skulls. A third had been divided with slabs and its contents layered: at the bottom was a pewter jug and plate decorated with a wheel. The head of a deity carved in local stone – bald and smooth with recessed ears, round open eyes and a bland expression – was found on a platform inside a shrine located in a remote part of the grounds of a late Roman house. Perhaps it was used by the pagan employees of a Christian householder.

Caerwent Romano-Celtic Temple (*above*)

The fourth-century temple is unusual in having a cella with an apse on the north and ambulatory entered from the south. It stood within a rectangular temenos on the site of an earlier building containing a sacred pit. A long entrance hall was added on the south, and a priest's rooms and trinket shops faced the temple from the north (far side). Pagan ritual continued despite the advance of Christianity. Among many bronze votives in the cella were miniature tables, a snake, a mask and an eagle. A pipe-clay Minerva and Venus were also found, plus inscriptions to Mars Lenus and Mars Ocellus Vellanus, imported variants of the Roman god more concerned with healing than war. An octagonal temple in an oval temenos stood outside the town wall by the east gate.

Maryport, Cumbria

Below: *The platform, banks and ditches of the Roman fort seen from the east.*

A Roman road runs along the coastal ridge from a gap visible in the defences of Alauna fort. Victorian excavations in the fields north-east of the fort showed that a cemetery had developed along the course of the road in the second century AD. Burials in stone cists and under flat slabs, funerary monuments, the remains of pyres, including calcined bones, and many broken urns were found. The stone foundations of a 'temple' and 'circular building' were probably a mausoleum and monumental tomb. In 1870 seventeen altars were found in pits around the parade ground. Fifteen of them, for the First Cohort of Spaniards in garrison c. 122–38, show an altar was ceremonially buried, and a new one dedicated, every year

when the army renewed its vow of loyalty on the emperor's official birthday. In the third century the parade ground was moved south of the fort and a civilian settlement laid out, with some of the houses overlying graves of the former cemetery. The paved streets had sewers and the stone-built houses had external render painted pink, slate roofs, glass windows and tiled floors. The soldiers, their families and the native population created a cultural mix with a wide variety of

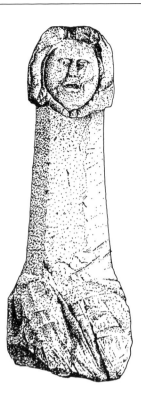
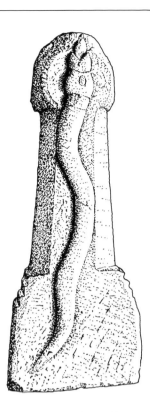

religious beliefs. Soldiers came from the Rhine, the Balkans and Spain. An Etruscan family put a carved stone pine cone over their tomb; a Greek dedication to Aesculapius, god of medicine and healing, was made; an altar in Roman form was dedicated to the local Celtic goddess, Setlocenia, by a man with both Roman and Celtic names. Altars were inscribed to Jupiter, Vulcan, Victory of the Emperor, and Neptune; small altars were used for private worship of household gods of prosperity, the Imperial Cult, Christianity, Mithraism and the cults of at least four Celtic deities were practised.

The Serpent Stone, Maryport (*above*)

From the cemetery came an extraordinary sculpture known as the Serpent Stone. Fashioned from an earlier monument, it has a crested serpent carved on the back of a pillar-phallus crowned by a Celtic severed head wearing a neck torc and shocked expression. It powerfully combines Celtic symbols with the Roman phallus of good fortune. Anne Ross (1974) believes the Celts used the severed head as a phallic symbol and only under Roman influence began to illustrate the phallus naturalistically. The fragmentary remains of another similar stone were found close by. There may be some connection between the Serpent Stone and the many representations of naked, horned figures with spear and shield – some with erect penis – found at Maryport. Is this part of a cult of a warrior fertility god, perhaps even Cocidius, as suspected at Yardhope?

Bartlow Hills, Linton, Cambridgeshire

The largest barrow in Roman Britain. Once part of a group of seven, now only four remain in a row. They are the burial mounds of an aristocratic, provincial family of Romanized native gentry, or Roman immigrants of Celtic extraction from northern France and Belgium, where similar flat topped tumuli are found. Cremated bones in glass vessels, along with exotic ritual objects and feasting utensils of decorated bronze, glass and pottery, were placed inside chests buried with iron lamps still burning. The quality of the artefacts, mainly imported from the Rhineland and northern Gaul, demonstrates the owners' high status. Items found in the 1832–40 explorations included an iron folding stool, with bronze fittings and a leather seat, of the sort a servant would carry for his master, perfume bottles and ornaments, bathers' strigils, glass jugs and Samian-ware bowls, remains of flowers and box leaves, a sponge, incense, and blood, milk, wine mixed with honey and other liquids. Slaves and the poor who could not rely on families to provide – joined burial clubs which bought and maintained modest monuments and plots on behalf of their members. They also arranged ritually complete funerals to prevent unhappy ghosts, holding the necessary commemorative feasts and celebrations on anniversaries of the death.

Lullingstone Roman Villa, Eynsford, Kent

One of seven Roman villas known in the fertile valley of the River Darent. Started around AD 75, it underwent many changes before being destroyed in a fire around 420. This 'deep room' was first built as a cellar: it had several different entrances and was remodelled over the years. A pit for ritual water was sunk in the centre, opposite a wall painting of three water goddesses in the niche of a blocked doorway. The central nymph has greenery in her hair and blue water streaming from her breasts. Later the steps at the north-west (rear right) were blocked off and two marble busts of eastern Mediterranean origin – depicting related bearded men wearing Roman dress – placed on the remaining 'podium'. In front of them four pots were sunk in the floor – one, a small beaker, painted with the word sweetness. A cult of ancestors was probably being practised, the pots being used to receive libations for the souls of the dead. Around 360 the rooms above this pagan shrine were converted to a Christian chapel and antechamber. The painted wall plaster featured protective Chi-Rho monograms – the opening letters of the Greek Christos – and male figures with arms stretched wide in the ancient attitude of Christian prayer called *orantes*. A family might have been hedging its bets, or maybe pagan and Christian worship was being practised simultaneously by different groups in the household. Similar ambivalence is displayed by earlier burials in a deep vault of the pagan temple-mausoleum on a terrace above the villa. A young man and young woman, in lead coffins embossed with scallop shells, were accompanied by pagan grave-goods, but the coffins were packed with gypsum – a practice of people expecting bodily resurrection. In the early fifth century, the plaster of the house-chapel collapsed into the cult room as fire raged and pagan Saxons ran riot in a Roman province abandoned by the legions.

CHAPTER THREE

THE AGE OF SAINTS

Y AD 410 the Romano-British had been left to fend for themselves and the official structure of the Roman Church based on urban bishoprics was beginning to falter. The Word was spread and kept alive by Celtic 'saints' travelling the western seaways – holy men and women having direct contact with continental centres of Christian culture and the British immigrants of Brittany. Inspired by the anchorite communities of Egypt, Palestine and Syria, Celtic missionaries embraced the austere concepts of the 'desert' to travel as martyrs for Christ, live as hermits and found small monastic communities under the authority of abbots rather than the Roman system of bishops and dioceses. Two of the earliest British saints, Patrick – born the son of a deacon somewhere in western Britain (probably Cumbria) who became the apostle of Ireland – and Ninian – apostle to the Picts – are described as bishops, but by the late 400s the simplicity and self-sacrifice of the monastic ideal, more suited to a tribal and pastoral way of life, had caught hold. Overwhelming personalities such as St Columba – a volatile mix of druid prince and Christian soldier – through force, conviction and personal example worked miracles of conversion, and created lasting sources of inspiration and wonder.

The early saints did battle with ancient spirits of place, often taking on their names and attributes and inhabiting their former sites of power, such as wells and caves. The lives of the saints – often copied out or rewritten by medieval monks – are full of pagan echoes and elements of Celtic folklore. Accepting Christianity did not always mean the abandonment of former practices. The Council of Tours in 567 suggested that those who worshipped trees, stones or fountains should be excommunicated. Through Irish missionaries, and Iona and its foundations, the Celtic Church was largely responsible for the conversion of the Anglo-Saxons of Northumbria and East Anglia. In 596 Pope Gregory sent the Italian-born Augustine and his companions to evangelize the Saxons of Kent. In 601 their king, Ethelbert – whose Frankish wife, Bertha, was already a Christian – was baptized. Gregory advised Augustine not to forbid and destroy all pagan rituals and temples but to insist worship was done in the name of the true God and feasting in honour of Christian festivals.

The increasing rivalry between the two churches was brought to a head at the Synod of Whitby, held in 664. The main argument concerned the calculation of the date of Easter, which involved a complicated reconciling of the lunar calendar, used to locate the Jewish Passover, and the solar or Julian calendar. Rome insisted that Easter must always fall on a Sunday (the day after the Sabbath), but by the Celtic method it could fall on any day of the week. This split was causing havoc at the Northumbrian court: King Oswy, following the Celtic tradition, often celebrated Easter while his Kentish wife, adhering to Roman rules, was still fasting for Lent. After a vigorous and passionate debate, Oswy decided against Iona on being told that Rome spoke with the authority of St Peter, who had seniority over St Columba. Not wishing to be barred by the keeper of the keys of heaven, Oswy committed England to the primacy of Canterbury, under Rome, while the Celtic Church retreated to linger in Scotland and Wales into the twelfth and thirteenth centuries. The influence of the Celtic Church continues, however, with its unofficial saints and holy places increasingly venerated.

Burghead Promontory Fort and Well, Moray, Grampian

Earthworks lie on a finger of land gesturing to the Moray Firth from the top of Burghead Bay. This view looks inland from the fort to where the modern town has destroyed the three lines of earthen ramparts defending the promontory neck. One of the largest forts in Scotland, around the fifth century AD this was a major centre of Pictish power. The Picts were a grouping of British Celtic tribes mixed with a more ancient native population, from whom they inherited the non-Celtic elements of their language and the custom of electing kings from the female royal line. The Romans considered the tribes beyond the Antonine Wall to be utter barbarians (that is, they put up a good fight and were not amenable to Roman culture), dismissively nicknaming them Picti – 'Painted Ones'. Usually interpreted as a reference to tattoos or body paint, it may have been a general comment on their use of images – perhaps even the enigmatic symbols which the Picts later began to record in stone. Around thirty slabs, finely decorated with Pictish motifs, were

recorded from the fort, but only six powerful carvings of Pictish bulls have survived. Elements of sun worship survive in the midwinter fire-festival, during which a *clavie* – tar barrel – burns for luck on a scorched and blackened remnant of rampart called the 'Doorie Mound'. An underground rock-hewn chamber with a basin cut in the floor, seeming rather elaborate for a simple water supply, may have played a part in the ritual life of Burghead before Christianity took over. It has been described as a water shrine, drowning pool, Roman well and/or Early Christian baptistery associated with the local cult of St Ethan.

Inset: *Crosses carved on the rock face (and stones now in Whithorn Museum) show the cave has been visited by pilgrims since at least the eighth century, when Galloway was under Northumbrian influence.*

St Ninian's Cave, Whithorn, Dumfries and Galloway

This cave is considered to have been used as a devotional retreat by St Ninian in the last years of Roman rule in Britain, *c.* AD 400. Writing 300 years later at the Northumbrian monastery of Jarrow, the Saxon monk Bede explains that the conversion of the idolatrous southern Picts was achieved by the preaching of Bishop Ninian, 'a most reverend and holy man of British race, who had been regularly instructed in the mysteries of the Christian Faith in Rome'. Ninian may have been a priest sent by the Bishop of Carlisle to minister to an existing Christian community. Bede says that Ninian set up his own episcopal see dedicated to St Martin of Tours (d. 397) called Candida Casa – 'the White House' – a church built of stone 'which was unusual among the Britons'. 'Candida' may have described the appearance of fresh masonry, pale plaster or whitewash, but it also had the meaning 'clothed in white' (Roman *candidati* seeking high office wore a loose-fitting white robe) and could have been used to signify the spiritual radiance of Ninian's foundation. The Anglian version of the name, 'Hwit-aern', eventually became Whithorn.

A Celtic monastic settlement developed famous for scholars and missionaries, then Whithorn became in turn the centre of an eighth-century Anglian bishopric, a Norse trading settlement and finally a medieval cathedral priory. St Ninian's shrine was internationally renowned, and visited by royalty, until pilgrimages were banned in 1581, and the church and monastery were suppressed.

St Ninian's Isle, Bigton, Shetland

With church dedications ranging from Shetland to the north of England, St Ninian has a reputation as a formidable missionary, but so little is known about him that even his conversion of the southern Picts cannot be confirmed and Christianity was not established in the Northern Isles until the seventh or eighth centuries. The far-flung 'foundations' must be the work of many 'Ninians' – successive missions over the years from different centres perpetuating his name. Excavations on St Ninian's Isle in 1958 uncovered the ruins of this medieval church, built over the chapel and graveyard of a Celtic monastery. Nearly thirty items of Pictish silverware had been buried in the chapel, in a larch chest with part of the jawbone of a porpoise – the dolphin was used as an early symbol of Christian faith. A broken cross-slab sealed the pit, and several Early Christian stones were found on the site, including an Ogham inscription, and shrine pieces carved with Pictish ornamentation. The treasure was probably concealed around 800, at the start of Viking attacks on Shetland. The isle is linked to South Mainland by a sand and gravel spit, or tombolo– a perfect location for those seeking solitude in a peaceful world, but no refuge from the pagan Norse.

Dunino Den,
St Andrews, Fife

A footprint and basin carved in the surface of a sandstone outcrop overhanging Dunino Burn are traditionally associated with pagan rituals and the inauguration ceremonies of Pictish kings. Rock-cut steps lead down a fissure behind the outcrop which has the look of a huge head with its mouth in the stream. The atmosphere of this green sunken world is enclosed, remote and ancient. On a hot day in June the air was sickly with the choking scents of stinkhorn (*Phallus impudicus*) and the excrement of dogs and inconsiderate campers. Water and wood pigeons formed an endless loop of sound. Melted wax and candle stubs surrounded the basin, and carnations floated on fetid water, home to a frog. Worn paths between cracks in the rocks lead to flat tops, one of which has a hole cut in it the size of a fist.

A Celtic-style cross (*inset*) has been carved on rocks facing west towards the burn. It resembles eighth-century High Crosses and preaching stations; the elongated side arms could represent metal extensions as fitted to some of the Iona crosses. Footprint stones and rock-cut basins were used by the Christian Scotti of Argyll, and missionaries such as St Rule and St Fillan were at work in Fife in the eighth century. Victorian copy, Dark Age relic, or more recent attempt to Christianize a pagan place?

Dunadd Fort, Kilmartin Valley, Argyll

By AD 500 groups of Gaelic-speaking Scotti from Ulster had established their own kingdom of Dalriada (Argyll) in western Scotland, with a stronghold at Dunadd, a plug of rock rising dramatically from the marshy valley floor of the River Add. Scots fought the Picts to north and east with mixed fortunes until, in 843, they formed a political union under the kingship of Kenneth mac Alpin. The symbolic centre of this new kingdom of Alba was at Scone (Perth), where High Kings were inaugurated on the Stone of Destiny, brought from Ireland, possibly via Iona. In 1297 the stone was stolen by Edward I, being used for coronations in Westminster Abbey until returned to Scotland in 1996. A basin and right footprint cut in rocks just below the summit fort at Dunadd were used by the Dalriadian kings. It was to Dunadd that St Columba and his companions came from Ulster in 563 to visit the king – his kinsman, Conall – prior to setting up a monastery on Iona. Tradition says that Columba, who had made previous visits to the area, wanted the island of Lismore, about to be claimed by St Moluag. Columba was outsailing him to be the first to land when Moluag cut off his little finger, throwing it on to the shore. In fury Columba cursed him, but had to find another location. Conall may then have suggested, and granted him, Iona.

Opposite: *The rock basin and footprint below the citadel. A glass-fibre replica protects the surface of the footprint rock.*

St Columba's Footsteps, Keil Point, Kintyre

At Keil Point on the south coast of Kintyre, two footprints are carved in the stone of a rocky knoll above a chapel dedicated to Columba, Kilcolmkil. The southern print (left) is ancient, associated with the Dalriadian Scots and claimed as the place where Columba first set foot in Scotland. A comfortable cave and holy well are in the cliff face to west and east. This was a landing-place from Ireland and the southern point of the kingdom of Dalriada. The footprint could have been carved to claim the land, as a territorial marker used for rituals of inauguration, landing and embarkation. An outcrop to the right has a socket for a wooden cross. In the distance is the thin, dark line of Ulster. Descriptions of medieval ceremonies for the Lords of the Isles have the chief elect dressed in white, with his foot placed in a carved print to show he would walk in the ways of his predecessors. He was handed a white rod symbolizing power to rule, reminded to use it wisely, then a Mass was said. In culmination and celebration, the assembled company, including the necessary bishop and seven priests, feasted for a week.

Iona, Argyll

St Columba (Columcille: dove of the church, church pigeon) was a Gaelic-speaking Irish Scot, born Colum MacFhelim MacFergus in AD 521 by Loch Garton, Donegal. His father and mother were of royal descent; his great, great-grandfather was Niall of the Nine Hostages. He was a poet, patriot, prince and warrior-priest. He loved the oak – 'crowded full of heaven's angels is every leaf of the oaks of Derry' – successfully cursed those who annoyed him, engaged druids in contests of magic, frightened off a monster in the River Ness, talked with angels, nursed injured cranes and was visited by a horse on his deathbed. The man and the stories surrounding him exemplify a world in which a fervent love of Christ often found pagan expression. Invoked in the Hebrides as *'a Chalumcille chairdeil, chaoimh'* – Columcille, the friendly, the kind – there is also a saying 'earth went over Odhran's eye', referring to the story of Columba burying alive his cousin to sanctify the infant monastery on Iona: 'It is permitted to you that some of you go under the earth of this island to consecrate it.' Odhran volunteered or was chosen by lot. After three days they opened the grave to find him talking: 'There is no such great wonder in death, nor is hell what it has been described.' Columba hurriedly ordered, 'Earth, earth on Oran's eyes lest he further blab.' At the age of forty-two he chose to leave Ireland in the 'white martyrdom' of exile for Christ. Rumours suggest he had been severely criticized for participating in, and partly causing, a bloody battle between Clan Niall and the High King.

Iona is a small, intensely beautiful island off the Ross (south-west peninsula) of Mull. In 563 Columba and twelve companions landed in a bay on the southern coast, now named after him. It was not the safest approach by sea, but he may have been directed by King Conall to someone living there who could help him. Odhrain of Latteragh (d. 549) had established churches on Mull, Tiree and Iona. There are stories of 'seven bishops' there who tried to get rid of him – 'false priests' whom he drove away. Iona has been claimed as a druids' isle with sacred yews, magical wells and pagan sculpted stones so it is possible that quite a lot of religious readjustment and rumour spreading was going on. Dùn Cùl Bhuirg, a small Iron Age hillfort by the north-west coast, became one of Columba's favourite haunts.

St Mary's Abbey (*left*)

The restored buildings of St Mary's
Benedictine Abbey, founded in 1200, seen
from Dun I, overlooking the Sound of Iona
to Mull and the distant mountains of Jura.
Columba chose this site for his monastery
on the north-east coast, where there is a
well, good land for arable and pasture, with
shelter from the western winds, and safe
landing-places. Columba's timber buildings
stood in the centre of a rectilinear earthwork
enclosure of 20 acres, the rampart or *vallum*
of which shows as a discoloured bank in
front of the abbey. St Oran's chapel is on the
extreme right, with a grassy hummock,
claimed as the site of Columba's cell, by the
cross immediately right of the abbey.

St Martin's Cross and Torr an Aba (*right*)

The east face of St Martin's Cross, west of
the abbey. An eighth-century High Cross
with serpent-and-boss panels showing a
fusion of art styles and stone-carving from
Ireland, the Pictish areas and Northumbria.
The stone was brought from Mid-Argyll; the
slots in the arms were for decorated metal
extensions. To the rear is Torr an Aba –
'Rock of the Abbot' – on top of which were
found remains of a small cell containing
clean beach pebbles and a rock-hewn bed.
According to Adamnan, his biographer,
Columba's cell was built overlooking the
Sound 'in a higher place than the rest of the
monastery'.

Cobhan Cuilteach Hut Circle (*below*)

Iona is about 3 miles SW-NE by 1 mile E-W. Across its narrow centre is a pass of fertile land linking the north-east coastal strip with the machair: the lime-rich, seashell grassland of the central western bay. In the south-west and north-west, away from the beautiful beaches, is a sombre landscape of gneiss outcrops divided by small glens of bog and moorland. In such a remote hollow lies a hut circle of uncertain date, possibly used as a hermitage or retreat. It may be the 'more remote place in the wilderness' to which Columba withdrew for prayer. He would also go alone to the western machair, to Sithean Mor – 'the big fairy hillock' behind the Bay at the Back of the Ocean.

One day, against strict instructions, a monk followed Columba to see him trysting with angels on the grassy mound.

Well of Youth (*right*)

At the foot of dark rocks below the summit on the northern side of Dun I is a pool known as the Well of Youth. Those seeking healing and youth of spirit should wash in its waters at dawn. To the north is the beach and small knoll called the Hill of the Seat, where Columba in his old age would go to sit. Vikings started attacking Iona around 800, the blood of monks staining the white beaches on at least two occasions. The remaining monks withdrew to Ireland and Iona was left abandoned.

Eileach an Naoimh Monastery, Garvellach Isles, Argyll

Holy Island, or Rock of the Saints, is the most southerly of the Garvellachs – four 'rough rocks' rising from the Firth of Lorne between Jura and Mull. The boat trip from Ardfern on Loch Craignish passes between the islands of Jura and Scarba: the infamous Gulf of Corryvreckan with its 'speckled cauldron' whirlpool. A tall underwater rock pillar in the deep narrow channel, combined with a flood tide and strong westerly wind, produces 20-foot-high water-spouts and a killer vortex. Little Corryvreckan, between Scarba and Lunga,

Below: This double beehive cell, near a pulpit-shaped natural rock, is of early Christian corbelled dry-stone design, but altered and restored using mortar.

is even more dangerous. Although rocky and often storm-locked, Eileach an Naoimh has fertile strips of land still used to fatten stock. With a supply of fresh water and sheltered areas for cultivation, it was perfect for Celtic monks – remote but not inaccessible, austere yet with a wild, intoxicating beauty. It is traditionally associated with St Columba, and believed to be the island of Hinba mentioned in his biography. Landing involves negotiating St Columba's harbour – a narrow rocky inlet on the south-east, leading to a tiny shingle beach with a holy well.

An underground cell called the prison (*right*) conjures ideas of penance and meditation, but it would also have been useful as a cold store. Nearby is the main domestic building of the monastery, with a garden enclosure, burial area and lazy-bed cultivation beyond. On the hill (rear left in the photograph), lies a circular kerbed enclosure with a cross-inscribed slab which marks the traditional burial place of Columba's mother, Eithne. Other remains include a Celtic chapel, a medieval church, a winnowing barn, a kiln for drying corn and beehive cells.

Covered in a layer of turf to keep out wind and rain, beehive cells (*left*) would have been a snug enough place to hide from storms. Adamnan describes an occasion when Columba was storm-bound on the island, staying in his cell for three days and nights, neither eating nor drinking. A bright light shone at night and 'the grace of holy inspiration was marvelously poured forth'. Obscure biblical passages were made plain and many things 'hidden since the beginning of the world' were revealed to him. On another occasion four saints from Ireland (Brendan, Comgall, Cormac and Kenneth) visiting Columba on Hinba decided he should say a 'Mass of the Saints'. As Columba stood at the altar, they saw a most luminous globe of fire burning over his head. When, after twenty years of anticipation, I visited the island on a glorious June day, it was being used as a campsite for a sailing tour, and under siege from a flotilla of yachts – just like the old days!

Llantwit Major, St Illtud's Church, South Glamorgan

The earliest monastery in Wales was founded by St Illtud – 'most learned of all the Britons' – sometime before AD 500 at Llantwit Major (Llanilltud Fawr). It was an important missionary centre, with a school internationally famous for its Christian knowledge and teaching. Students were divided into twenty-four groups to enable worship to continue throughout the day and night. The ninth-century crosses shown below now stand on the site of the old Celtic church.

Nothing remains of the original monastery beside a stream in this sheltered, fertile valley near the coast. The west church (left in the photograph ab ovc) is a fifteenth-century remodelling of a Norman church built on the site of the Celtic original. The east church was built in the thirteenth century for the canons of the medieval monastery. For the founder of such an important and long-lived Christian centre,

little is known for certain about St Illtud, descriptions of his life being full of wonders and contradictions. He may have been born in Brittany and taught by St Germanus of Auxerre, but there are stories that he was a soldier converted in Wales who, in a poignant early morning scene, sent away for ever his wife after resolving to found a monastery. It was St Dyfrig (Dubricius) who prepared him as a monk and marked out the monastic enclosure. Illtud drained land for cultivation and introduced an improved form of plough. He was assisted by a tame fawn and a legend persists that a golden stag, looking west, is buried on the outskirts of the town. A villa to the north-west of Llantwit, abandoned after a massacre around AD 350, has been suggested as St Illtud's original abode as a hermit.

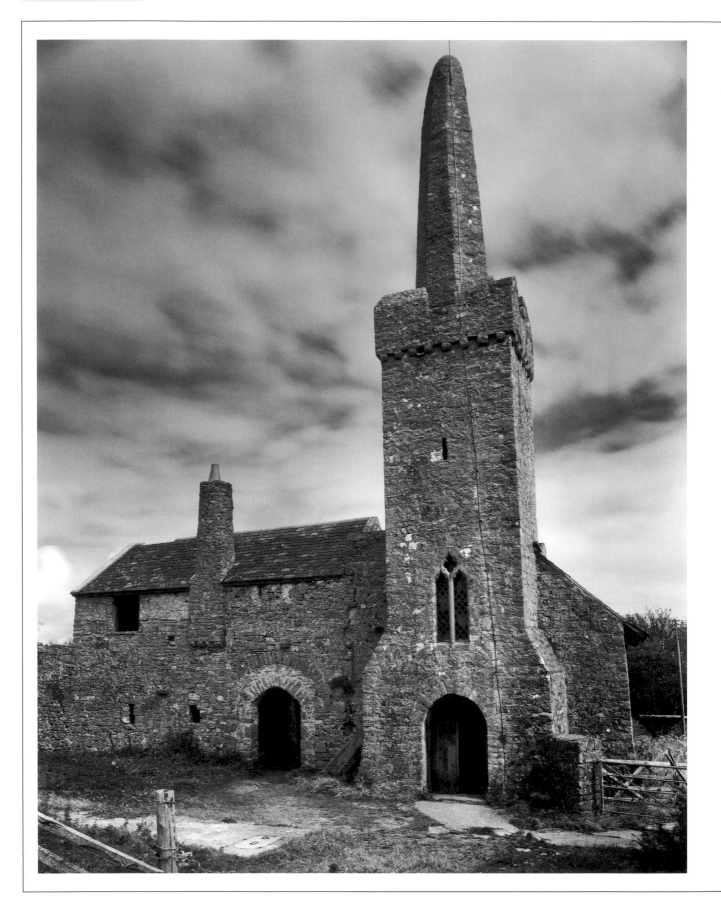

Caldey Island Priory, Dyfed

St Illtud, along with St Dyfrig, has also been credited with founding the first monastic community on Caldey Island, 3 miles south of Tenby. Certainly he had close links with the island: one of his pupils, St Samson, who went on to found the monastery at Dol in Brittany, was a monk at Caldey and was appointed by Dyfrig as the second abbot. The pre-Norse name of Caldey was Ynys Pyr – 'the island of Piro' – and a life of St Samson claims that this Piro was the first abbot, describing his unseemly death by falling one night into a deep well when drunk.

Restored remains of the medieval priory (*left*) include the gatehouse and St Illtud's Church, with its western tower. Inside the church is an Ogham slab of c. AD 500 with a cross and Latin inscription; various attempts at translation have included the names of Dyfrig, Illtud, Cadwgan and Jesus.

A stained-glass window (*right*) depicts Illtud as a monk and as a knight of King Arthur, told by an angel to return to the holier life of his youth.

A new monastery built between 1910 and 1913 is now home to an order of Reformed Cistercians. The island is a true holy place, fragrant with spirituality and gorse flowers, used by the monks to make perfume.

Steep Holme Island, Bristol Channel

Gildas, the Celtic historian and saint, was born in Strathclyde but moved to Wales as a family man before becoming a monk with St Illtud at Llantwit. St Gildas and St Cadog of Llancarfan would retire for Lent to the islands of Steep Holme and Flat Holm in the Bristol Channel, but were disturbed by pirates. At the age of forty-three, *c.* AD 520, after much travelling he settled down to write *De Excidio et Conquestu Britanniae* (*The Ruin and Conquest of Britain*), for which he is primarily known.

In the style of an Old Testament prophet, Gildas berates clerics and five British kings for their low moral standards, explaining the Anglo-Saxon incursions as divine retribution for the sins of the British. It is Gildas who first tells of the 'arrogant usurper' (later generally known as Vortigern) who disastrously invites Saxon mercenaries into Britain to fight the Picts and Scots. He also describes Ambrosius Aurelianus – a Briton with a Roman name, one of the inspirations for the King Arthur legends – who won a great, but not final, victory against Saxons at Mount Badon, near Bath or in the Wiltshire/Dorset area.

Towards the end of his life Gildas withdrew to an island monastery in Morbihan, Brittany. His last request was to be placed in a coracle and pushed out to sea – a reminder of pagan Celts journeying to the Isles of the Blessed beyond the setting sun.

Dinas Emrys Fort, Beddgelert, Gwynedd

The 'City of Emrys' is the traditional location for a story told about Vortigern by the ninth-century writer Nennius. Forced to flee from England by the Saxons he had hired, Vortigern's wizards advised him to build a fortress on this precipitous rock beside the River Glaslyn. Each night the building work of the day before disappeared. The advisers declared that only the sacrificial blood of a child without a father would break the spell. A suitable boy, Ambrosius (Emrys the Overlord), was brought to the site, whereupon he outwitted the wizards by explaining that the tower was being built on a hidden pool in which would be found one vessel inside another, separated by a white cloth. These were discovered and the cloth opened to reveal a red dragon and a white dragon, who awoke and began fighting. Eventually the red dragon chased the white one away, Ambrosius interpreting this as the native British people having the final victory over the Saxons. He declared that he, not Vortigern, was destined to reside on the hill. Emrys has been identified both with Merlin and with Arthur. Excavations discovered fifth–sixth-century occupation debris, including shards of eastern Mediterranean pottery, and structures around an artificial pool in the centre of the site. The base of a rectangular stone tower, and a cistern built within the pool, are from the later castle of a Welsh prince.

Burry Holms, The Gower, West Glamorgan

Hermits seeking solitude in the wilderness were drawn to the very places where the old gods lingered. Caves, megalithic tombs, abandoned forts, sacred springs and hidden valleys were all chosen by saints who took on some of the attributes of the spirits of place; they also inevitably attracted followers, robbers and murderers. Islands were ready made 'deserts', and ancient symbols of holiness lodged deep in the Celtic psyche. St Kyned (Cenydd), the son of Gildas, 'made a cell among the rocks of Gower'. A small tidal island off the north-west coast of the peninsula had been used as a promontory fort and occupied in the Roman period. At the sheltered mainland end are remains of a medieval ecclesiastical settlement called St Kenydd-atte-Holme. The stone buildings were erected on the site of huts and a timber church within a barrel-shaped monastic enclosure or cashel. St Kyned also founded a monastery at nearby Llangennith. An ancient well is outside the church gates, which are carved with some of the more fantastic scenes from the saint's legendary life. Born a cripple in Brittany, he was set adrift like Moses, but came safely to an island where he was taught and protected by angels, eventually becoming a hermit. St David cured him but, displeased, St Kyned asked for his deformity to be restored.

Right: The 'City of Emrys sits on a summit defended by rough stretches of walling, linking crags and out-crops, and forming a Dark Age citadel.

St Finnan's Isle,
Loch Shiel, Highland

An island in the western part of Loch Shiel, between the Highland areas of Moidart to the north and Sunart to the south. It might have been named after a local hermit or was possibly founded by disciples of one of the two sixth-century Irish abbots, St Finnian of Clonard or St Finnian of Moville, who studied in Scotland. Still used as a burial ground, there are grave markers spanning 1,300 years: the earliest are mossy piles of rounded stones and river pebbles; the most dramatic, several megalithic slab-crosses overlooking the jetty. Slight signs of a bank enclose the highest ground, on which stands the ruin of a long rectangular church containing a stone altar with a crucifix and chained handbell. A carved skeleton lies on a grave nearby and rough slabs dot the southern slopes, which are covered in broom and encroaching blackthorn. A deer had swum the loch and lain down to die among the bluebells.

Puffin Island and Penmon Priory, Gwynedd

The island off the south-east tip of Anglesey has many names: in English it is Puffin Island, but the birds were wiped out by rats eating their eggs; it is Priestholm in Norse, because of its monks and hermits; in Welsh it is Ynys Seiriol, for the sixth-century saint who established a monastery there and at Penmon. The remains of a church with a twelfth-century stone tower stand within Seiriol's monastic enclosure. The tower had been built against a small memorial chapel over the burial of a muscular man of late middle age. It is also known as Ynys Lannog, after the father of Helig ab Glynnog, wicked ruler of the fertile land now submerged in Conwy Bay. During drunken festivities at his court he and his family, down to the fifth generation, were overwhelmed by the sea. There is no access to the island, but at Penmon a holy well, Viking-period crosses and the fish-pond, church and other buildings of an Augustinian priory can be seen on the site of Seiriol's monastery.

Inset: St Seiriol's Church and Penmon Priory buildings, including a dovecote of c. 1600, seen from the south-west.

St Blane's, Kingarth, Isle of Bute

Bute is a comfortable island dangling in the mouth of the Clyde, sheltered from the west by Arran and Kintyre. St Blane's monastery is in an idyllic setting – unless the Vikings have just landed – near the southern tip. A Romanesque church stands within the upper graveyard, retaining the oval shape of the original cashel or monastic enclosure of Irish type. A handsome wayfaring tree and wild cherries cluster around the western gateway to this upper churchyard. The secondary lower churchyard contains the foundations of a chapel. Both enclosures have medieval and earlier burials marked by overgrown slabs and low Celtic crosses. The stone-faced earthen bank of the monastic *vallum* survives particularly well on the north, where there is an entrance. A circular structure, known as the Cauldron, stands in the compound's north-western corner, where the *vallum* meets the cliff. Looking like a massive Iron Age hut circle, its function is unknown. The early monks could have built a 'strong house' in traditional style, or taken over a pre-Christian settlement. Other remains include a Viking hog-backed tombstone, a well, a basin carved in a boulder, and the foundations and enclosure of a sixteenth-century vicar's manse. St Catan (Chattan of Kingarth) established the monastery in the sixth century, after migrating from Ireland and founding several churches in the Clyde area. When his sister Ertha gave birth to a son of unknown father, in a rage Catan set her and the newly born Blane adrift in an oarless boat, which eventually washed ashore on the Ulster coast. More restained versions of the story say that St Catan sent the young St Blane to Ireland to be educated by St Comgall at Bangor. After seven years Blane 'the mild' returned to be reconciled with his uncle,

eventually taking over as abbot of the monastery and bishop of the surrounding area. He finally went as a missionary to the eastern Picts, his best-known foundation being at Dunblane, north of Stirling. St Blane's thrived until two abbots were killed in Viking raids in the eighth century, and the Norse settled on the site for a while. In 1204 the monks of Paisley Abbey were granted the church and lands of Kingarth.

St Nectan's Kieve, Tintagel, Cornwall

The Trevillitt river flows through an enchanted glen associated with the firstborn of St Brychan's 'twenty-four' children. A 60-foot waterfall has hollowed out several rock basins, the most recent being known as St Nectan's Kieve. Around AD 500 Nectan established his hermitage above the falls, hanging a silver bell in the tower to warn sailors. According to local legend, he and the bell are buried at the base of the falls, but Hartland (Devon) was the centre of his medieval cult, holding his relics until the shrine was destroyed at the Reformation. In the Hartland legend he is decapitated by robbers who have stolen his cows. Nectan picks up his head and carries it back to his hut beside a spring. A cottage (the Hermitage Tea Rooms) was built on the chapel ruins in the mid-nineteenth century, a time when writers such as Wilkie Collins were making romantic visits to the glen, descending rock-cut steps in the footprints of earlier pilgrims.

Roche, Cornwall

This chapel dedicated to St Michael was built in 1409 over a partly rock-hewn cell on the granite outcrop of Roche Rock. The site has been used by hermits since early Christian times. One story concerns a leper whose daughter, St Gundren, used to fetch him water from a well (now lost) which ebbed and flowed with the tide. Inevitably the site also features in Arthurian legends, on this occasion as a refuge or prison in the story of tragic and fatal love between Tristan, nephew of King Mark of Cornwall, and Iseult, his uncle's wife. To the rear right is the Parish Church of Roche, dedicated to St Gonand, a male saint venerated in the thirteenth century.

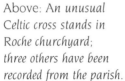

A 'divination' well (*below*) situated in a small, wooded valley north of Roche is known as St Gundred's (or St Conan's) Well. Bent pins were dropped into the water by girls wishing to know or influence their future. It was also said to cure a wide range of ailments, especially those of children's eyes. Strips of cloth are tied to the branches of nearby trees.

Above: An unusual Celtic cross stands in Roche churchyard; three others have been recorded from the parish.

Partrishow, Abergavenny, Powys

In the sixth century AD St Issui settled at a spring by the Nant Mair stream, which flowed east to join the river Grwyne Fawr. A missionary and healer, he was found one morning murdered in the well. A roadside slab incised with a Maltese cross marks the pathway. Just before the Norman Conquest, a wealthy leper cured by the water gave gold for the building of a church uphill from the spring.

The church (*above*) has a deep peace and many unusual features, including a pre-Conquest font, wall-paintings, texts and dyed memorials, side altars in the nave, and a rood-loft and screen of Irish oak, decorated with winged dragons. St Issui may be buried, under a stone altar bearing six consecration crosses, in a chapel on the site of the original church at the west end of the nave. In 1188 Archbishop Baldwin, accompanied by Giraldus Cambrensis (Gerald of Wales), preached the Third Crusade at the churchyard seats and cross south of the nave. The parson stabled his horse in a small building west of the church.

St Non's Well, St David's, Dyfed

St David was born near this well on the spot now marked by St Non's Chapel. Named after his mother, the spring appeared at the very moment of David's birth during a violent storm. Visitors drawn to its miraculous healing powers were so numerous and proved to be so lucrative that an attendant lived close by. A stone roof covered the well and surrounding benches, where pilgrims rested or underwent cures. Into the 1800s children were regularly dipped and votive offerings of such things as pins and pebbles were made. The well was restored and rededicated in 1951.

St David's Cathedral, Dyfed

The present cathedral church of St Andrew and St David, standing on the site of the sixth-century monastery, was begun in the 1180s and heavily restored in the late medieval and Victorian periods. The Bishop's Palace to the left is mainly fourteenth century. To the rear right is the peak of Carn Llidi, where David used to go to converse with angels. The original monastery of Tygwyn, where St David was educated and became abbot, was on the lower slope of Carn Llidi, above Whitesands Bay. He moved the community further

inland to this more secluded site beside the River Alun, in the 'valley of the little marsh'. The wife of Boia, a brigand and 'druid' who lived in a small fort (Clegyr Boia) to the south-west, was so determined to drive away the monks that when other ploys failed she sacrificed her stepdaughter. Taking the girl to gather hazelnuts, she dressed or shore (cut) her hair, then cut her throat, pouring innocent blood on the ground, where up sprang a fountain of clear water. This having done no good, she ran away. The following night Boia was killed in his bed by Irish pirates. The monastery became famous for its learning and asceticism, David practising many austerities such as frequent genuflexions and total immersion in cold water. He and his monks wore animal skins, had a strict diet of bread, vegetables and water, and undertook heavy manual labour, pulling their own ploughs. So severe was the regime that his steward, cook and deacon tried to poison him. On another occasion the steward tried to murder Aidan, David's favourite disciple. A hot-headed Irish saint on a visit struck and killed the boy assigned to wait upon him. David died around 589, his relics being kept in the monastery. The first church was burnt down in 645. Between then and 1097, the monastery was attacked, burnt or destroyed over a dozen times. Bishop Morgenau was killed by Vikings in 999 and in 1080 Bishop Abraham met the same fate. Around 1090 the site was described as abandoned, the shrine stripped of valuables and masked by undergrowth. The first Norman bishop was enthroned in 1115, when, in a political move to weaken Welsh autonomy, the Celtic monastic organization of the cathedral was changed to the ordinary diocesan type. David has been regarded as the patron saint of Wales since 1123, when Pope Callixtus II officially approved his cult and conceded, because of the dangers of the journey to Rome, two pilgrimages 'to seek David' should be equivalent to one to 'seek the Apostles'. Despite many setbacks and disasters, Christian worship, prayer and pilgrimage have taken place in this valley for over 1,400 years.

Reliquary of St David and St Justinian

At the Reformation, St David's thirteenth-century shrine, the stone base of which survives between the choir and presbytery, was stripped of its jewels, ornamental wooden canopy and murals. The relics, which had stood on the shrine in a portable casket, were taken away. During the restorations of 1862–77, a walled-up recess was found in Holy Trinity Chapel, at the back of the high altar. It contained the mixed bones of a very tall man and a short one. The remains, now in a modern casket, are believed to be those of St David – 'a tall, dignified man' – and his confessor, St Justinian.

Carn Ingli, Newport, Dyfed

Like his friend and contemporary St David, Brynach the Irishman conversed with angels. St Brynach lived as a hermit for a while on Carn Ingli, known as the 'Mount of Angels', where heavenly companions ministered to his needs. He may have made a home within the summit hillfort, or periodically ascended to pray and gaze on Ireland. St David's work was hampered by pagans, and a strange episode in Brynach's life may be a memory of similar resistance. Legends relate that he was married to (or desired by) Corth (or Cymorth), the daughter of a Welsh chieftain. Because of his missionary activities (or rejection of her), she paid men to kill him but he escaped to wash his wounds in a well since known as the Red Spring. He established a church at Nevern, where an important group of early Christian memorial stones keep company with a magnificent Celtic cross of *c.* 1000. Nevern was on the pilgrim route from Holywell in north Wales to St Davids; a cross and praying station are carved in a cliff off the Frongoch road, west of the church.

St Melor's Well, Linkinhorne, Cornwall

The tangled life of St Melor, conflating several individuals and locations, manages to pack in many elements of pagan Celtic folklore. Melor may have been a Breton saint who came to live in Britain, or whose relics were taken from Brittany to Amesbury (Wiltshire) by the Saxon king Athelstan. Also strongly associated with Cornwall, he was venerated at Mylor Churchtown, Merther, and his renowned healing spring, marked by a medieval well house, at Linkinhorne. The basic story hinges on the relationship between a young Christian prince and his pagan uncle, who cuts off the child's right hand and left foot after killing his father. The uncle hopes to rule, as Celtic law prohibits a maimed king. Melor is sent to a remote monastery and supplied with a silver hand and bronze foot, which by the time he is fourteen function as well as the originals. Hearing of this, his uncle induces Melor's guardian to behead him. On his way to the uncle, the murderer, nearly dying of thirst, is advised by Melor's head to thrust his staff into the ground. A fountain gushes forth and the staff takes root, becoming a beautiful tree bearing fruit. The uncle touches the head and dies three days later. The Cornish tradition has a British prince, Melorus, and a Breton bishop, Mylor, buried together at Mylor, their graves marked by a cross carved from a pagan monolith with a sun symbol at its head. In the Wiltshire version, Melor's remains are brought to Amesbury by wandering monks who place his coffin on the altar, where it becomes miraculously fixed and the monks are forced to to leave without their precious burden. This story casts much light on the origins of Celtic saints and the competition for relics and patrons.

Chittlehampton, Devon

Heathen hostility, severed heads and holy wells are recurring themes in stories of Celtic saints. Urith or Hieritha was a Christian maiden beheaded by haymakers with their scythes at the instigation of her pagan stepmother. A stream sprang up as her head struck the earth and the dry ground was decked with flowers. A slab from the well on the traditional site of her martyrdom (around AD 700) can be seen set into an alcove next to Rose Cottage, at the east end of the village street. The legendary circumstances of her death are almost identical to those of St Sidwell at nearby Exeter. Although the only dedication in the world to this obscure local saint, Chittlehampton was a popular place of pilgrimage, offerings to Urith's shrine paying for the tall west tower. The shrine stood in the high arched recess

immediately north of the altar. Her image was removed from the church in 1539; the empty niche was painted blue and inscribed to her memory in 1764. Urith's body is believe to remain in the church, buried beneath the passage leading to the vestry or under the ancient tomb slab in the recess. A carving on the stone pulpit of *c.* 1500 shows the saint holding a palm of martyrdom and the church foundation stone, or a book of her acts and miracles. A modern statue, in a niche on the south face of the tower, depicts Urith carrying a scythe and a 'second' head.

Holywell, Clwyd

Other stories feature virtuous maidens decapitated by amorous pursuers, healing waters pouring from the earth at the touch of their blood. The most famous of these is Gwenfrewi (Winefride of Holywell), beheaded in AD 660 by her spurned suitor Caradoc, as she ran for the protection of St Beuno's chapel. Beuno reunited head and body, bringing her back to life – a service he reputedly performed for others, including the daughter of the king of Gwent. He turned Caradoc into a pool of water which sank into the earth. Gwenfrewi went on to become abbess at Gwytherin, in the Conwy valley, where she was buried, her relics being removed to Shrewsbury Abbey in 1138. Part of the gable end of her eighth–ninth-century reliquary from Gwytherin, originally a triangular-shaped wooden box covered with ornamental metalwork, has recently been located at Holywell by Tristan Gray Hulse. In 1416 Henry V and his retinue made pilgrimage on foot from Shrewsbury to Holywell for ritual cleansing, and in thanks for Winefride's aid at Agincourt.

The present twin-level chapel was built around 1500 by Lady Margaret Beaufort, mother of Henry VII. The crypt forms a well-chapel, where the spring rises before flowing into a long rectangular pool in the courtyard. Tall pillars support a vault decorated with scenes from Winefride's life. The inner pool is star-shaped, with five recesses in honour of the well at Bethesda, where Jesus healed the sick. Pilgrims would pass through the water three times, in memory of the ancient Celtic baptism rite of triple immersion, in the belief that St Winefride would answer prayers by the third time. Very frail and infirm pilgrims would be carried through the pools on the backs of friends. The well was also used to divine. A man accused of eating a stolen goat was brought to the well, where he denied his guilt, but the goat 'gave forth a bleating in the belly of the thief'. The well survived the Reformation and determined attempts made in the seventeenth and eighteenth centuries to suppress pilgrimages and drive out the Catholic priests. Pilgrims of many persuasions visit the well and, despite the severing of the original water source by mining in 1917, the cures continue.

Glastonbury Tor, Somerset

A conical hill held sacred to the primal mother, topped by a church tower dedicated to St Michael. Rival influences are also revealed in the story of a sixth-century hermit and the king of Annwyn, the Celtic underworld. According to a medieval account of his life, St Collen had a cell in a secret place under a rock on the flanks of the tor. Overheard describing as demons those who lived on the summit, he was called to account for his lack of respect by Gwyn ap Nudd. Climbing to confront the king, St Collen found a magnificent castle and a host of fair people. Refusing the proffered 'food', declaring, 'I will not eat of the leaves of the tree', he threw holy water in all directions, reducing the scene to a bare hillside. Excavations on the summit have found Dark Age remains of drinking, feasting and metalworking. The same medieval life of St Collen also has him fight and kill a 'Giantess of the Pass' who was preying on humans in the Vale of Llangollen (Clwyd) and duel with a Saracen in the presence of the Pope. The natural slope of the hill has been terraced by medieval farming, but some of the ridges may be prehistoric; the remains of a ritual pathway ensuring ascent was in the form of a spiral. An encircling serpent was the symbol of the coiled natural energies of earth and sky, and the Church usually counteracted such forces in high places with a dedication to Archangel Michael, slayer of dragons.

Left: *The Tor and Whitelake rhine (watercourse) from the north-east.*

Burgh Castle, Norfolk

The Roman Saxon Shore fort of Burgh Castle was given to St Fursey, for the establishment of a monastery, in AD 633 by Sigebert, King of the East Saxons. Fursey and his companions – Irish monks who had left their homeland as pilgrims for Christ – were largely responsible for converting the pagan East Anglians. Bede describes the famous visions of the afterlife granted to Fursey at Burgh. On falling ill and entering a trance, Fursey fled his body from sunset to cockcrow, seeing choirs of angels and hearing the songs of the blessed. Three days later he again withdrew from his body, being escorted by angels to heaven to learn joyful and sorrowful things from angels and saints. His way to heaven was obstructed by devils cunningly using the thoughts and deeds of his life to make accusations against him. At one point he is shown the four fires – falsehood, covetousness, discord and cruelty – which will consume the world. Assured by angels that the innocent will not be harmed, Fursey is shocked on being burnt; having once accepted some of the clothing of a man who had died in his sins, Fursey must share his punishment. When Fursey awoke, he had on his shoulder and jaw a permanent scar where the evil spirits had thrust against him the burning sinner.

Holy Island, Northumberland

Oswald of Northumbria defeated Cadwallon, Christian King of Gwynedd, ally of Penda, the pagan Saxon King of Mercia, at the battle of Heavenfield, fought beside Hadrian's Wall in *c.* AD 634. The miraculous victory of an inferior and largely heathen force was attributed to Oswald's prayers at a wooden cross he erected before the battle. Oswald had become a Christian while in exile on Iona and requested a missionary from them to help convert his kingdom. Colman, stern, impatient and inflexible, returned to Iona, declaring that the Angles were an obstinate, ungovernable race of barbarians. A monk graced with discretion and prudence was sent as a replacement. With companions from Iona and Oswald's help, St Aidan established a Celtic monastery of wattle huts surrounding a thatched church on the tidal island of Lindisfarne. Aidan preached, often with Oswald acting as interpreter, founded monasteries and churches, and bought free Anglo-Saxon slaves to be educated for the Church. Missionaries trained by Aidan travelled throughout Britain, including St Cedd, who evangelized Essex from his base at Bradwell-on-Sea. Lindisfarne thrived – Cuthbert, the sixth bishop, being the best-known cleric – until the Danish raid of AD 793. Vikings attacked the island, killing cattle, priests and monks, 'raiding on all sides like stinging hornets and ravening wolves'. In 875 the monks fled the island, taking with them their rich store of relics, including the body of Cuthbert and the skull of Oswald, who had been killed by Penda. Cuthbert's body finally rested at Durham in 1070. By 1100 Benedictine monks were building the present priory, which was

abandoned at the Dissolution in 1537. A modern causeway links Holy Island to the mainland, but the ancient direct route, for saints and sinners alike, was straight across the mud-flats to Chare Ends, along a line marked since 1860 by wooden poles. Every year at Easter modern pilgrims, some carrying wooden crosses, walk – with faith and an eye on the tide – barefoot across the sands.

CHAPTER FOUR

CONTINUITY AND REVIVAL

HIS FINAL CHAPTER gives examples of survival, into the Middle Ages and beyond, of beliefs and patterns of behaviour which can be broadly regarded as 'Celtic', and the current revival of Celtic dimensions in Christianity, personal spirituality and environmentalism. Just as Celtic newcomers to Britain absorbed many of the ways of the earliest inhabitants, so Celtic thought coloured Roman worship and gave a particular flavour to Christianity. Contrary to what I was taught at school, the Anglo-Saxons did not drive out of 'England' all of the 'Romano-British' so that 'Celts' were to be found only in what became Cornwall, Scotland, Wales and the Isle of Man. Evidence from settlements and burial grounds in England show Britons and Anglo-Saxons coexisted in separate enclaves and mixed communities cemented by intermarriage. The pagan Saxons of Mercia formed an alliance with Christian Britons of north Wales against the Angles of Northumbria. Regulations for Britons are included in the seventh-century laws of King Ine of Wessex. By the eighth century obvious skeletal differences between ethnic groups were diminishing and English society was forming out of the mix. This was dealt a devastating blow in 1066 by the Normans, who seized control of Church and state, the law and the land, and made Latin and French the official languages. The 'English' are hated for damage done to the 'Celtic' areas of Britain, but much was the work of Norman descendants who also suppressed English noble families and culture.

Science believes matter is neither created nor destroyed. Perhaps it is the same with ideas, whizzing around like lottery numbers until it is time for them to pop out again. Certainly pagan Celtic practices survive, and the medieval cult of relics had more to do with Celtic and Saxon folk-beliefs than with biblical teachings. Into this century in East Anglia, Celtic rituals and ancient potions were being used to successfully control horses and influence agricultural processes. Throughout Britain cattle plague was treated by driving the herd over one of their number buried alive. In Christian communities horses were blessed in church and at wells, and in some cases sacrificed. Bulls were slaughtered in honour of saints and madness was cured by a mixture of pagan and Christian rites. Hills, trees and stones were feared and honoured. People, cattle and milk were bewitched, only to be cured by water from a sacred lake. The four great Celtic calendar festivals of Samhain, Imbolg, Beltain and Lughnasa continued to be celebrated under Christian guise, but often with a pagan spirit. Wells used regularly into the 1800s for cures and cursing are being visited today and offerings made. During the Reformation relics and images were swept away in favour of the Word whose throne, the pulpit, eclipsed altar and rood to become the focal point of church worship. In many Anglican churches the niches again have images and incense is in the air. Pilgrims are on the march and Celtic Christianity is being seen as a way to a more vital and direct relationship with spirituality. The mystical traditions of many religions are coming to the fore, mixed with guilt and frustrated longings for the natural world. *Hiraeth*, the traditional yearning of the Celtic soul for a golden age, or perfect otherworld, is being mixed with ideas of a soul in everything and the fear we have allowed technology to grow faster than our ability to use it responsibly. Places of ancient sanctity are in use again and something is stirring. It could just be millennium fever or an overdose of *The X Files*, but realization of error, a sense of sterility in modern life and genuine hunger to experience a world beyond the material may be breaking through.

Mizmaze, Breamore Down, Hampshire

Mizmaze is an old dialect word for mystification, a labyrinth or place full of intricate windings. The turf and chalk maze on Breamore Down is considered to be prehistoric in origin – a place for ritual dancing, symbolizing concepts connected with fertility and the passage of spirits to and from the otherworld. The maze, sharing its hilltop with a round barrow, is in an area of Celtic fields, with Giant's Grave Neolithic long barrow to the south-west. The medieval Church sponsored a revival in use of labyrinths around the thirteenth century to illustrate the journey through life of the human soul and the path to salvation. In continental cathedrals (the most notable survival being Chartres) maze patterns were set into the floor, while in Britain turf mazes were constructed and restored. The chalk path would be followed to the centre and back, sometimes by penitents crawling on hands and knees. The maze lies in a wood of yew, ash, oak, hazel and whitebeam, which heightens its air of mystery and seclusion. Grasses, wild flowers and herbs crowd around the perimeter, with purging blackthorn lower down the hill.

Julian's Bower, Alkborough, Lincolnshire

British mazes were often named 'Troy Town', 'Walls of Troy' or 'Julian's Bower', in the belief that the funeral maze games of Helen's city were brought to Italy by Julius, said to be a son of Aeneas and the legendary founder of the Roman nation. Mazes are also associated with the story of Theseus slaying the Minotaur in the Cretan labyrinth. By Stuart times turf mazes were used more for sport than for ritual, and hedge mazes were becoming popular features in formal gardens. When first recorded in 1697, this maze at Alkborough was believed to be Roman. Its date remains unproven, although both prehistoric origins and cutting by the medieval monks of nearby Walcot have been suggested.

On the hilltop above, the Romans constructed an earthwork on the site of an earlier enclosure. The view north-west from the maze looks over the junction of the rivers Trent and Ouse as they combine to form the Humber – just the sort of location chosen for an Iron Age sacred site. Up to the last century May Day eve games were played along the raised paths of the dancing pattern. In November 1995 the maze was reseeded and sprinkled with lawn sand after a year of heavy wear which included use as a bicycle track by local children.

Wing, Leicestershire

At 40 feet in diameter, the maze at Wing is the same size as Julian's Bower and probably shares the same sequence of a prehistoric ceremonial site being reused in the Middle Ages.

Meavy, Dartmoor, Devon

Meavy Oak is claimed to be the last dancing tree in Devon, older than the Norman church and a pagan focal point around which the villagers whirled on May Day eve and other festivals. Information in the church states that the tree was planted as a gospel oak to accompany the church in the time of King John. Trees and dancing can be tricky subjects for modern Christians. Tree Dressing Day, initiated by the environmental charity Common Ground, came under criticism for 'enduing' trees with spiritual qualities, and perpetuating medieval occultism by dancing around them. Liturgical dancing in Hereford Cathedral – by women priests using an Israeli folk-dance to 'own' the church for women who had been held away from it – was similarly frowned upon as New Age paganism. Dancing the hallelujah was considered acceptable, but weaving a mystical sacred circle was worshipping the wrong god. Meavy Oak has certainly been danced around, forming the heart of the community for centuries. It shares the village green with the War Memorial, which stands under an oak planted in November 1920 and bears the inscription: 'Behold this stone, set up under an oak, By the Sanctuary of the Lord, Shall be a witness. Joshua XXIV. 26.27.'

Alderley Edge, Cheshire

Water issuing from a groove falls, in an arc of drops blown by the wind, into a carved stone basin. A sketch in Christina Hole's *English Folklore*, published in 1940, shows the basin unbroken and the author states that crooked pins were still being dropped into the 'wishing well'. The small chamber hollowed out of the rock beside the basin was warm and snug on a bitter March day; it has a curved ceiling grooved with pick-marks. This and an adjacent rectangular basin are now called holy wells, but the ancient springs, heathland and woods of the 600-foot-high sandstone escarpment were frequented 'when God were a lad' and Christ just a glint in his eye. Copper was mined in the Bronze Age at Stormy Point nearby and bronze palstaves were deposited in springs or pools in the area.

With rocks and trees taking expressive forms, Alderley Edge has a sense of otherness which is a magnet for tales and legends. Arthur and his knights are reputed to lie asleep in a hidden cave, further west along the cliff, beside Merlin's Well, which is another rock spring filling a stone trough, with the weathered face of a wizard on the outcrop above.

Virtuous Well, Trellech, Gwent

A pagan spring Christianized by dedication to St Anne, the well at Trellech gained its present name as a result of its medicinal virtues. Traditionally there were nine wells fed by four separate springs, each capable of curing a different condition, such as scurvy or colic. As late as the seventeenth century, pilgrims were regularly visiting the well, resting on the stone seats, bathing in the outer pool, drinking from the cups provided and placing offerings in the niches. The water bubbles and glugs under modern slabs, which have raised the outer floor level, almost hiding the seats. Small pebbles used to be carefully placed in the water and wishes made: many bubbles indicated a wish granted, a few signified a delay and no bubbles meant a refusal. A farmer once closed up the wells, but 'a little old man' appeared and informed him that he would lose the water on his own farm as a punishment. The fairies were said to dance at the well on Midsummer eve, drinking water from the picked harebells found scattered every Midsummer morning. Ferns, liverworts and wild strawberries grow in the walls of the well; strips of cloth hang from the hazel trees. Flowers and other offerings are still made. On my last visit a sachet of incense from an ashram in Pondicherry (India) was floating in the water.

St Clether, Launceston, Cornwall

The pre-Conquest chapel was rebuilt in the fifteenth century, restored in 1895 and rededicated in 1909. Water runs from the well house through the eastern end of the chapel, under the altar and out through the south wall. A sunken area to the south of the altar was used for baptisms and healing. St Clether's relics were kept in a recess just above the channel to give the running water supernatural power. Pilgrims used the relic-charged liquid from the well in the southern wall, leaving their thanks offerings on a shelf to be collected from inside the chapel by a priest. The universal medieval belief in the power of relics does not seem to have been warranted by Scripture so much as earlier folklore, and pre-Christian veneration of skulls, ancestral bones, charms and fetishes.

St Clether (Cledarus) the Aged, one of the many children of saintly King Brychan of south Wales, came to settle in this sheltered valley of the River Inny, building his chapel and cell beside a spring.

Llaneilian, Anglesey

St Eilian was a Cornish or Breton missionary who landed with his family and animals on the north-east coast of Anglesey, establishing a religious foundation and reputation for miraculous cures. The present parish church has a Norman west tower and pyramidal spire, with nave and chancel rebuilt in the late 1400s. St Eilian's chapel of the 1300s is connected to the chancel by a later passage. His well on the coast to the north-west was much visited, especially on the eve of his feast day (13 January), when the water would be drunk and prayers said in the well chapel. Afterwards, placing a groat in the oak chest in the church would obtain a blessing on

cattle and corn, and cure such ills as agues, fits and scrofula. The chest, dated 1667 and studded and barred with iron, still stands in the church, while the panelled wooden base of the shrine survives in St Eilian's chapel. The large sums donated enabled the purchase of two farms whose rents were used for the upkeep of the church. In the eighteenth and nineteenth centuries the offerings were used for poor relief. Even a holy well could be made to curse and harm with the use of bent pins and the victim's name on paper or a stone. A wax figure was found in the well, pinned to a small decorated slate scratched with five sets of initials. It was believed that an impaled frog, floated in the well by attaching corks to the ends of the skewer, could cause an enemy misfortune for as long as the frog stayed alive. By the end of the 1700s another well of St Eilian, near Colwyn Bay, had become invested with the most terrible power for evil: it was widely believed that a person cursed there could be made to suffer and die. Money was paid to the custodian and a name was written on paper, which was fixed with a bent pin and placed in the well to do its work.

St Gwenfaen's Well, Rhoscolyn, Anglesey

The well on the cliffs in Rhoscolyn parish is altogether more benign, being considered to cure, or prevent, mental disorders in return for two white spar pebbles placed in the water. The use of white pebbles and quartz in funerary and ritual contexts dates back in Britain at least as far as the Neolithic. White pebbles were placed in early Christian burials and used as 'turning stones' on altars and cross-bases. The wishing ritual at many wells includes the use of white stones. Quartz and rock crystal were believed to give drinking water a 'magical potency'. Gwenfaen is the patron of Rhoscolyn Church, but as the name means 'white stone' and there is no agreement on the gender or date, a 'saint' could have grown out of the ritual or white stones used in honour of an elusive hermit with a shining name. The well is in three parts: steps lead down to a flag-floored ante-chamber with stone corner seats; the enclosed well, flanked by apsidal recesses is next; then there is an open pool with three steps on either side. Water trickles over the notch in a vertical slab and flows away to the cliff in a stone-lined channel.

St Fillan's Pool, Tyndrum, Scotland

Up to the early nineteenth century a dramatic cure for madness was practised in Strath Fillan. The mentally ill were thrown from a rock into a deep, still pool beside the north bank of the River Fillan (Dochart). They were then taken to St Fillan's Chapel, where his bronze bell (the Bernane Bell) was placed over their heads for a few moments before they were left overnight tied to the font. If found free in the morning, they were considered to be cured. The priory of Augustinian canons was founded in 1317 by Robert the Bruce, who believed that the relic of Fillan's luminous left arm had helped him defeat the English at the battle of Bannockburn. The pool, which lost its healing power when a bull was flung into it, is now used for swimming and picnics. The swirl is alder pollen moving on the surface of the water.

St Non's Well, Altarnun, Cornwall

The mother of St David is believed to have settled for a while at Altarnun, where church and well are named after her. The holy well feeds a bowssening pool, which was used in a cure for madness. The Reverend Richard Polewhele, in his History of Cornwall, compiled 1803-8, describes unfortunates being tumbled into the pool by a sudden blow to the chest, and then tossed up and down. The violent immersions were accompanied by prayers and sacred chants until the patient was exhausted, and the 'fury' abated. The patient was carried to the church for a vigil, when 'certain masses were sung'. A similar pool used to exist behind the fifteenth-century well chapel and cross in the village of St Cleer on Bodmin Moor, to the south of Altarnun.

Isle Maree,
Gairloch, Highland

The island of St Maelrubha floats in sight of Slioch, on the surface of Loch Maree, like a fairy mound. It is a sacred isle where lunacy cures were practised and bulls were sacrificed to the saint who partly replaced a pagan god. The cure took various forms over the years, but included rowing the patient three times sunwise around the island, jerking him three times into the water on the end of a rope. Soaked and confused, victims were made to kneel in the ancient enclosure before the altar (or the tree stump that replaced it) from a ruined chapel, then to drink from the healing well, where an offering was fastened to a sacred oak. More immersion followed, the process being repeated over several weeks until success or despair was achieved. So many nails (to fasten rags, bone buttons, buckles, etc.) and coins were hammered into the Wishing Tree – a practice popularized by the 1877 visit and writings of Queen Victoria – that it turned into a scaly serpent, dying of copper poisoning. The well was dry in 1860 and the tree nearly dead by 1886. Bleached limbs are now propped over the dry hollow and thoughtless visitors are doing harm to living trees nearby. St Maelrubha, an Irish missionary who founded a monastery at Applecross, on the coast opposite Skye, died in the early 700s. His evangelization of the northern Picts required considerable compromise: taking over ancient sacred sites, he allowed continuation of pagan practices in a Christian context. In the seventeenth century the results of this ambiguity were of great concern to the ministers and elders of the Dingwall Presbytery. They record the folk of Applecross and Strath Carron sacrificing bulls to their 'god Mourie'. In 1678 four men ritually killed a bull for the health of one of their wives. Other heathen practices cited and deplored were the veneration of wells and other superstitious monuments, the ritual circling of ruined chapels, offerings of milk poured on the hills and people trying to fit their heads into a holed stone to divine the outcome of a journey. Into the nineteenth century cockerels were sacrificed to banish epilepsy and as a cure for cattle murrain (foot-and-mouth) one of the herd would be buried alive. In 1164 a bull was sacrificed to St Cuthbert on his feast day at his church in Kirkcudbright. On the ridge above Strathlachlan by Loch Fyne (Argyll) a large stone known as the Old Woman of the Thunder was considered to be an earth goddess. A minister wrote in the 1790s that 'the people paid her a superstitious veneration, and were under dreadful apprehensions of her anger'. On Isle Maree the sacrifice of bulls continued openly into the eighteenth century. This happened on many occasions, but particularly in August at the feast of Lughnasa, the pagan Celtic celebration of first fruits as the harvest began which is now the Christian festival of Lammas.

Pistyll, St Beuno's Church, Nefyn, Gwynedd

Lughnasa was a major festival under the patronage of the Celtic god Lugh (Lugos). The Gauls celebrated the feast on 1 August in the god's own city of Lyon, until the Romans claimed the festival, and the month, in honour of Augustus, their deified emperor. In Britain under the Anglo-Saxons it became *hlaf-maese*, loaf-mass or Lammas Day. The first ears of corn were plucked, ceremonially prepared, baked and shared. The pagan gods – later the names of Mary Mother, the Trinity and the saints – would be invoked, their praises sung and circuits walked sunwise for the protection and success of the anticipated harvest. The whole community played a part, with large gatherings held at prominent ancient sites and on high places such as Silbury Hill (Wiltshire) or Mow Cop (Cheshire). These celebrations developed into the wakes and fairs held around late July and early August. At Pistyll on the Lleyn peninsula, St Beuno's Church is decorated and loaves are placed on the altar on the nearest Sunday to 1 August. Rushes are strewn and herbs and plants gathered from the churchyard and surrounding area: teasels, bulrushes, sea holly, heather and ling, fennel and wormwood, montbretia, rowan branches with berries, camomile, cow parsley, rosemary, wild hops and more. The church is also dressed at Christmas and Easter. Pistyll was a halt for pilgrims *en route* to Bardsey Island. It had a monastery, an inn and a hospice growing its own medicinal herbs. Beuno, reputedly buried under the altar, may have founded the site in the seventh century, but Clynnog Fawr, further north, was the centre of his cult – the location of his well and shrine. In 1589 a visitor witnessing the sacrifice of a bullock to St Beuno at Clynnog was told that the local people dared not cut the graveyard trees 'lest Beyno should kill them'

Bardsey Island, Gwynedd

By the twelfth century Bardsey Island, off the south-west tip of Lleyn, was firmly established as a place of pilgrimage. Pilgrims came by boat from south Wales, through Snowdonia or down the north coast from Holywell, calling at a network of chapels, inns, wells and hospices. Such was the attraction of the island that many chose to be buried there, some being brought by boat from the mortuary chapel at Mwnt in Cardigan Bay. The belief that 20,000 saints are buried on Bardsey may have arisen from a misreading, as Roman numerals, of some of the capital letters on a grave inscription to Senacus the priest. Bardsey is associated with St Cadfan, who founded (or attended) the Celtic monastery in the sixth century, and Dyfrig and Deiniol, who are said to be buried there. Only a tower and later graveyard remain on the site of the thirteenth-century Augustinian priory. Many bones and long cist graves were disturbed in the 1800s when building work was undertaken nearby.

Lord Newborough had 'model' farm units built in the 1870s. One is used by the Bardsey Bird and Field Observatory and the rest by the Bardsey Island Trust, who have owned the island since 1979 and arrange for limited visits. Healing and spiritual retreats are held, along with yoga and self-development courses. Others go on personal pilgrimages, to help with conservation work, study the wildlife and enjoy the peace of a miniature kingdom. The heady mixture of isolation, spartan conditions, spirituality and the natural world can be imagined as close to that of the Celtic saints.

Looking south-west from Mynydd Mawr to Bardsey Island

St Mary's Well, Aberdaron, Gwynedd

Fresh water bubbles up in a crevice at the bottom of cliffs on the mainland opposite Bardsey. Ffynnon Fair is reached by a dangerous path, down steps and across slippy rocks, from the tiny cove below Trwyn Maen Melyn. Traditionally an embarkation point for pilgrims, it is far too dangerous to have been used regularly as there are safer options from beaches in Aberdaron Bay. Up to the 1950s, when visiting the mainland, inhabitants of Bardsey would go to drink and collect water from the spring, which is fresh and sweet, even when just uncovered by the tide.

Boleigh Fogou, Lamorna, Cornwall

Fogous (earth houses or souterrains) are something of a mystery. These artificial 'caves' with long stone-lined passages and small chambers are usually found in association with Iron Age huts and defended homesteads. The fogou at Boleigh stands within a contemporary enclosed settlement and has a small 'creep passage' running north-west from the main passage near its entrance. Claimed as ritual structures, storage cellars, refuges and escape runs, their functions have so far eluded positive identification. Some examples in Ireland do run from inside a hut to outside a fort. Trip-stones at foot and head height, sudden twists and turns, forked passages and confusing chambers suggest evasion and flight, but many just look like dead-end death traps. Tacitus describes the Germans hollowing out underground caves, covering them with manure and using them as storehouses and refuges from winter frosts. He also claimed they hid in their boltholes to escape detection by raiders. Some believe that the fogous, deliberately constructed to collect natural energies, were used as places of ceremony, spiritual training and initiation, much as the underground kivas of Native Americans. They could also have been used for forms of incubation or sacred sleep, as practised at Romano-Celtic healing sanctuaries. Whatever their original purposes, fogous do function well as 'isolation tanks' where everyday consciousness may be stilled and, in the mystical tradition of all religions, a different type of awareness achieved. This fogou, standing in the garden of the Centre for Alternative Education and Research, is used during courses on personal and spiritual development.

Ffynnon Gwenlais, Llandybie, Dyfed

An ancient yew, recently dated to around AD 500 and long regarded as protector of the valley, stands at the source of the River Gwenlais. It and the holy well have been at the heart of recent campaigns to protect Carmel Woods and the Gwenlais valley, described as the 'Welsh Glastonbury, a place of immense spiritual, cultural and historical importance'. Rich in legends and ancient remains, the valley, with its rare wildlife, ancient woods, extensive cave systems and ephemeral lake (turlough), has been under threat from plans to expand old quarry workings. Local residents and conservation bodies fought the plans but the Secretary of State for Wales decided a 1948 permission, granted as part of the post-war industrial drive, was still valid. This has now been challenged and activities are to be confined to existing quarries, which over the last 100 years or so have destroyed cave systems, burials and other important archaeological remains. The future of the only known turlough in mainland Britain is uncertain because of an open-cast coal-mining application. The Green Movement has been derided, as a form of new paganism, for seeking to question the belief that the best way of creating wealth is to destroy 'worthless' things which are truly irreplaceable and beyond price.

Glastonbury Tor, Somerset

A virtual island floating in a sea of marsh and mist, the Tor (*opposite*), ripe with symbolism, acts as a focus for so many beliefs: a Neolithic goddess mound with spiral maze; a hollow hill, entrance to the otherworld; hub of a giant landscape zodiac; Avalon, haunt of King Arthur; the New Jerusalem, walked upon by Jesus and Joseph of Arimathea, guardian of the Holy Grail. Glastonbury is the 'ism' capital of Britain, where nearly every alternative item is available and all fashions are catered for. Vans and 'benders' fill secluded copses along the rhines radiating from the town, and tents in the apple orchards below the tor are checked each morning to ensure the inhabitants survived the night. Glastonbury is a very special place, but I found the the current wave of grimly determined seekers of meaning somewhat dispiriting.

Chalice Well, Glastonbury (*below*)

The wrought-iron well cover was presented by Frederick Bligh Bond as an offering for peace after the First World War. Two circles represent the interlocking worlds of substance and spirit, forming the central *vesica piscis* or the sacred fish, used as a symbol for Christ.

St Oran's Chapel and Iona Abbey, Argyll

On a site originally founded by Columba, Benedictine monastery buildings abandoned at the Reformation are once again home to a religious community. The Iona Cathedral Trust, established by the Duke of Argyll in 1899, has the increasingly expensive responsibility for conserving and maintaining the religious buildings. Restoration of the cathedral ruins was organized between 1938 and 1965 by the Trust's tenants, the Iona Community, founded by the now Very Rev. Lord Macleod of Fuinary. Through youth programmes, working visits and retreats, they ensure that there is life and worship at the abbey all year round. This Church of Scotland Community, dedicated to a life of Christian witness and mission, has had a great influence on modern worship, promoting an informal style of service full of music and spirit. The contrast between those living, working or staying on the island and the frenzied day visitor is dramatic. John Smith, the former Labour Party leader, is buried in the graveyard of St Oran's Chapel. In 1995 the enthusiasm of up to 1,000 visitors a day was such that surrounding graves collapsed, headstones were trampled on and his plot had to be fenced off.

Most of the rest of the island is in the care of the National Trust for Scotland which endeavours to maintain its special qualities. Despite tourism stressing the island – to misquote Dr Johnson – a person is little to be envied whose piety does not grow warmer on Iona.

Bradwell-on-Sea, Essex

At the invitation of King Sigebert, St Cedd and his companions established a monastery at the Roman fort of Othona, overlooking a landing-place in the Blackwater estuary mud-flats. Becoming Bishop of the East Saxons in AD 654, Cedd reused Roman stone and tile to construct a cathedral chapel astride the fort's western gateway. St Peter's-on-the-Wall stands at the end of a Roman road trodden for centuries by those seeking a flavour of Celtic mysticism in this most English of counties. St Peter's is often celebrated as a Celtic foundation because Cedd was trained at Lindisfarne by Aidan of Iona. But St Cedd was Northumbrian-born, accepted the authority of Canterbury and Rome, and built a Byzantine-style church of stone with an eastern apse, porticos, and a western porch. The chapel – used as a barn in the seventeenth century, reconsecrated in 1920 by the Bishop of Chelmsford – forms the focus of the annual diocesan pilgrimage.

Bare and simple, the seventh-century nave has a beautiful quality of light and serenity, enhanced by services and meditations of the nearby Othona Community, and prayers of visitors increasingly drawn to the individual spirituality and earthy wisdom of the early Church. The modern altar incorporates stones from Lindisfarne, Iona and Cedd's monastery at Lastingham (North Yorkshire), where he died of the plague on a visit in 664.

The barn-like interior of St Peter's-on-the-Wall is a receptacle for light and essence.

St Non's Well and Chapel, St Davids, Dyfed

Above St Non's Bay, on a site considered numinous since prehistoric times, standing stones share the field with a medieval chapel honouring the place where St David was born. The chapel contains an early creed stone incised with a Latin ring cross. The altar table was a stone grasped and imprinted by St Non in the throws of labour. Beyond is the holy well – scene of wonders and miraculous cures and the goal for centuries of pilgrims and penitents.

The Passionist Fathers restored and rededicated the well in 1951, building a Shrine to Our Blessed Lady beside it. On the hillside above, a chapel built in a Celtic style in 1934 stands before St Non's House, run by the Passionist Congregation as a centre for spiritual renewal. Specializing in missions and retreats, they are vowed to preaching the love and mercy of God as manifested in His passion and death on the cross.

Pennant Melangell, Llangynog, Powys

Melangell's church lies at the head of the haunting and remote Tanat valley. Established as a place of sanctuary in the seventh century, in recent years it has flourished again as a centre of Celtic Christianity, offering healing, counselling and prayer. The daughter of an Irish king, St Melangell fled from an arranged marriage and lived in Cwm Pennant without human contact for fifteen years. Brochwel, a prince of Powys, was out hunting when his dogs chased a hare into a bramble thicket. He found the hare sheltered by a beautiful young woman rapt in prayer. The dogs retreated howling and the huntsman's horn was fixed to his

lips. Deeply impressed by Melangell's demeanour and piety, Brochwel granted her the valley as a perpetual refuge. Melangell stayed for the rest of her life, a community of holy women forming about her. A stone church was built around 1160, with an eastern apse over Melangell's grave, and her relics were placed in a Romanesque shrine. A sanctuary protected by law, those seeking healing, refuge and forgiveness made generous donations at the shrine until it was broken up in the sixteenth century. From then on the Norman church underwent many changes. The apse was replaced by a square structure and pieces of the shrine were built into the walls of church and lychgate. In extensive renovations between 1988 and 1992 the reassembled shrine was put back in the chancel. The square-ended building was taken down, a new apse being built on the twelfth-century foundations of Cell-y-bedd – 'the room of the grave'. The slab believed to have marked Melangell's original grave is set in the apse floor. Thanks to the continuing work of St Melangell's Guild, the valley is once again the goal of pilgrims and a source of inspiration.

St Columba's Cave,
Knapdale, Argyll

This green, airy cavern is claimed as Columba's first landfall on his way from Ireland to Iona (via Dunadd) and the first foundation of his Dalriadan mission. Just above a small bay in Loch Caolisport, with fresh water close by, it is a perfect place to shelter. Mass used to be said here and ecumenical services are still held. The floor is kept clean, the entrance being fenced against sheep which congregate in the coolness of the neighbouring cave.

The ancient stone altar is decorated with plants, flowers and offerings of coins, pebbles, quartz, pine cones, orange peel, shells, wax and candles. A cross is carved above the altar and there is a basin-like depression in the rock just inside the entrance. At the rear of the cave rotten steps lead to a damp alcove full of beach stones, broken shells, bones and dark earth. On the path up from the beach there is a ruined chapel, and a stream and small waterfall to the left of the cliff . On a hot June day the surrounding area was in bloom with yellow flags, *Rosa rugosa*, foxgloves, huge poppies, *Olearia macrodenta*, yellow *Buddleia globosa* flowers, azaleas and climbing white *Hydrangea petiolaris*. Sheep close-cropped the grass among flags on the rocky shore, while seals lay sunbathing on an islet (Eilean na h-Uamhaidh) in the mouth of the bay.

Holy Island, Lamlash Bay, Arran

This rugged island (*right*), once the home of an Irish saint, is now owned by Buddhists from the Tibetan Monastery of Samyê-Ling in Eskdalemuir (Dumfries). In the seventh century St Molaise (Laserian or Lamliss) lived in a rock shelter above the western shore.

Pilgrim crosses (*above*) and Norse runic inscriptions have been cut into the roof. By the 1100s a monastery had been founded – near the present pier on the north-west of the island – to act as hospice for the many pilgrims visiting his hermitage. Excavations in 1908 removed occupation debris, lowering the floor level below built-up deposits outside. The cave became a home for wild goats but is now used as a Buddhist shrine, swept clean with a broom of twigs. Offerings of leaves, stones, incense and a bowl of rice are placed beside a text draped over a stone. The area below the cave shows signs of 'sacred landscaping': large slabs of rock form 'altars' and 'seats'; stone steps lead to flat-topped rocks, perfect for contemplation; distinctive stones are placed in crevices; the well channel is lined with slabs; and unusual pebbles are placed in the stream bed. Litter is regularly collected from the shore, and everywhere is demonstrated a love and respect for natural forces and forms. Beside the path, leading to the retreat centre at the lighthouse complex, boulders are adorned with paintings of Marpa and Milarepa, Buddhist gurus of great holiness, teachers of enlightenment through meditation, whose ascetic lives had much in common with those of the early Christian saints.

Ippollits, Hitchin, Hertfordshire

One of only two churches in England dedicated to Hippolytus (loosed horse), the Roman priest and anti-Pope martyred in AD 235, torn apart by horses tied to his limbs. Sick horses were brought into his shrine through the north door in the hope of a miraculous cure. Horses were also taken to be cured and blessed at the well at Llansant Sior (St George, Clwyd), where water was sprinkled over their backs with a prayer said to St George. According to Lhuyd, writing in the 1690s, horses were also sacrificed there, one being given to the parson. In 1185 Giraldus Cambrensis published an account of the contemporary inauguration ceremony of an Ulster clan. In veiled but horrified terms, he describes the king-elect behaving as a wild beast in the presence of a white mare, which is then slaughtered and boiled. The king laps and bathes in the broth, while he and the assembled company eat pieces of meat.

Well of the Heads, Loch Oich, Highland

Over the spring of Tobar-nan-Ceann is a monument commemorating a seventeenth-century event with pagan overtones. In 1663 Alexander MacDonald, the Chief of Keppoch, and his brother Ranald were stabbed to death by rivals within the clan. After two years of delay, letters of 'Fire and Sword' were finally issued against the murderers, who were hunted down at Inverlair, killed and decapitated; their headless skeletons were uncovered a century ago. The heads were washed in the well before being presented at the feet of MacDonald of Glengarry, put on display at Invergarry Castle and then on the gallows at Edinburgh. Further elaborations of the story take on the imagery of Celtic folk-tales: on becoming noisy and restless – grinding like stones on the rocks in a storm – the severed heads were taken out of their basket and washed in the well to calm them. The monument erected in 1812 has 'portraits' of the seven heads surmounted by a hand holding a knife. The pompous inscription, glossing over the MacDonald's delay, praises the 'swift course of feudal justice'.

Druid's Temple, Ilton, North Yorkshire

The general availability of published classical texts in the sixteenth century, along with the beginnings of serious field archaeology, led to a love affair with the ancient Britons (or Celts as they were coming to be called in the early 1700s) which finally forced druids and megalithic monuments into an arranged marriage. Inspired by the excellent work of John Aubrey, published in 1695, but seizing on only one of his tentative suggestions, William Stukeley in the 1740s forged the false link between Stonehenge and druids which still colours popular misconceptions. Up to the early eighteenth century the prevailing attitude towards the druids was objective and unromantic, with scholars seeking parallels for the nobility and brutality of Celtic society in such groups as the American Indians. Stukeley and others put an end to this, turning the druids into Old Testament prophets with every rude lump of stone their handiwork. Aided and abetted by artists such as William Blake, the romance grew; our isle of Albion became the original Holy Land and a past golden age was simultaneously glimpsed, celebrated, mourned and longed for. Writers, artists and poets were setting cloaked, bearded figures in wildly romantic landscapes; town developments such as the Circus at Bath were based on the plans of prehistoric monuments; stone circles and burial chambers were restored and improved; and megalithic follies constructed.

At Ilton in the 1820s William Danby of Swinton Hall built a 'druid temple' with a ground plan loosely based on Neolithic examples in Malta. It has a Mycenaean-style tholos tomb dug into the hill, with a stone table, seats, sacrificial altar and Stonehenge trilithons thrown in for good measure. Sadly, the original grove of oaks has been replaced by insipid larches and pines. Arrangements of large stones lurk among the trees, and a tall column of stacked slabs forms an artificial Cheesewring on an outcrop above the temple.

Tigh nam Bodach, Glen Lyon, Tayside

'The House of the Old Man' sits in isolated Gleann Cailliche – 'the Old Woman's, or Hag's, Glen' – west of the northern arm of Loch Lyon. Inside the small dry-stone structure is a collection of strangely shaped river stones known as the 'Mother and her children' or the 'Family'. Volcanic swirls and ripples have been worn by water to resemble hips, waist and shoulders, or body, neck and head. The stones have no definite shape but the melted forms are compelling, having a sense of life and movement. The Mother in particular has an air of great significance, of potential power held ready in a squatting stance. The children are said to grow; a new one appearing every 500 years or so. Of uncertain age, the house was connected with the ancient pastoral practice of transhumance. Cattle, sheep and goats were taken to graze on the summer pastures of upland glens, where the women, children and a few young men and women of the community would live in shielings (summer dwellings, huts) to tend the animals, while making vital winter supplies of butter and cheese. The move was usually made in May, with a return to the home fields to help with the harvest around the end of July. Belongings and utensils were carried or carted, while the cattle were driven with great ceremony accompanied by songs. Pagan and Christian elements combined in charms, invocations and prayers to protect and bless the herds. The shielings were cleaned out, roofs of branches, turf and thatch were renewed, a lamb was 'sacrificed', a simple feast prepared and a blessing invoked. One of the first tasks at Gleann Cailliche was to place the family of stones in the grass to enjoy the summer sunshine and to thatch the house with rushes. In autumn the thatch was removed and the 'Family'

returned to a house covered by a roof of stones plugged with moss to keep out wind, rain and the snows of winter. When land use 'improvements' put an end to trans-humance, responsibility for the house was taken over by the keepers, stalkers and shepherds of the estate. The well-being of the valley is believed to depend on proper treatment of the stones, but after the recent retirement of the last guardian in his eighties, the tradition appears to be weakening. A genuine pagan Celtic survival or a more recent 'charm' perhaps grown out of a children's game? Whatever the origin, the stones are quite remarkable: their assembly and honouring have played an important part in the life of Glen Lyon, which is renowned for the variety and longevity of its ceremonies and customs.

The Dowloch, Penpont, Dumfries and Galloway

In the sixth century Gregory of Tours describes in his *In Gloria Confessorum* the annual Gallo-Roman festival at Lake Gévaundan in the Cevennes, which went on for three days. Animals were sacrificed and votive offerings of bread, cheese, beeswax, rags and clothing were thrown into the water. Annual meetings continued at the lake until 1868. In *The Statistical Account of Dumfries-shire*, published in 1841, the Minister of Penpont parish describes the legend of the Dowloch (Black Loch), which was considered to possess extraordinary 'virtue' (potency) in the healing of disease. The water, reputed to cure every malady, was especially renowned for treating cattle subjected to the spell of witchcraft. A deputy was sent carrying part of the dress of the ailing person, or furniture of the animal bewitched, as an offering to the spirit of the loch. The chosen person drew water in a vessel without letting it touch the ground, turned around sunwise, threw the offering over the left shoulder, then carried the water back to the patient without once looking back. The journey had to be undertaken in complete silence, ignoring any other person; if someone met on the road acted in a silent, unfriendly manner it was considered that they 'had been at the Dowloch'. Mr Murray, the minister, who died in 1736, used to refuse the sacrament to those who had engaged in the heathenish practice. Into the 1800s votive offerings of clothes and parcels of food were seen floating on the loch and scattered around its banks. An artificial lake in the grounds of nearby Drumlanrig Castle, named Park Loch on a map of 1855, has come to be known, confusingly, as Druid's Loch.

The charmed water of the Black Loch is now a brooding area of marsh, willow and alder scrub in a forestry plantation.

Madron Well, Penzance, Cornwall

A spring rising north-west of Madron village flows through a small twelfth-century chapel and baptistery built on pre-Norman foundations. Services and christenings are still occasionally held in the roofless chapel, which was used by Wesleyans in the eighteenth and nineteenth centuries. Considered especially good for curing skin diseases, the well was also used for divination. In 1641 a man who had walked on his hands for sixteen years regained the use of his legs after spending a night on the altar and then bathing in the stream. The spring retains its healing reputation: the tree above is hung with rags and other such tokens as clothes, tissues, plastic bags, sweet papers, socks, a baby's bib, plaited rushes, hair ribbons, handkerchiefs, threads of wool and clothes pegs.

Craigie Well, Avoch, Black Isle, Inverness

The Craigie Well is probably the most ancient and authentic of the clouty, or rag, wells around Inverness and the Black Isle. Its seclusion and difficulty of access preserve its atmosphere, ensuring that it is visited mainly as an act of devotion rather than as a tourist outing. The spring, emerging from a niche under a sloping lintel, trickles down to the shore of Munlochy Bay, leaving mud and greenery in its wake. The approach to the spring is wet and slippy, with a strong smell of sulphurous rot rising from the mud. Although Christianized as St Bennet's Well, it is in origin a Beltain (Celtic festival of 'bright fire') clouty well, still visited as a mark of respect on May Day, when coins and clouties are offered, wishes and vows pronounced.

The custom of leaving strips of cloth at wells is found in many countries. It may represent the former practice of shedding clothing as a way of casting off sickness. Gradually a strip of underclothing or the dressing of a wound was substituted. Some believed an affliction could be rubbed on to material and left behind, hung on a tree or buried beside the well. Rags, wool and human hair were also used as charms against sorcery, and as tokens of penance and fulfilment of a vow. The earliest reference found by Francis Jones to a rag well in Wales dated to the eighteenth century. In Scotland, Christ's Well at Mentieth was described in 1618 as 'all tapestried about with old rags'.

Munlochy Well,
Black Isle, Inverness

The clouty well beside the A832 is a startling and, to some, distasteful sight. Ease of access has made it a tourist circus, but this grotesque and disturbing scene has some of the atmosphere of pagan Celtic sanctuaries and the shrines of medieval Europe. Think back to the healing centres of Britain and Gaul, with their carved votive limbs and organs cast into the water and propped up in shrines, coins and silver feathers hanging from trees, and newly skinned heads nailed to temple walls. Go into Swiss churches in remote valleys such as Saas-Fee and gaze

upon rows of carved wooden arms and legs. Visit Lourdes, or go to Spain to kiss the Black Madonna encrusted with jewels and centuries of spittle. Thousands of knotted rags smother the trees and collapsing fence around the modern basin and spout. Items of clothing knotted together form long garlands trailing from branches. Some of the offerings speak eloquently of personal suffering, and the many items of children's and baby clothes seem heartfelt. A yellow anorak hangs from a branch 15 feet off the ground; shirts and jumpers are fastened to the torsos of trees; hankies, socks, towels and trainers turn in the breeze.

The original spring, issuing from a small cave uphill from the road, was traditionally visited at any of the four major Celtic festivals. Beltain, on May Day – the start of the lightest half of the year – and Samhain, on the night before November – the start of

St Mary's Well, Culloden, Inverness

Long used as a healing well, the 'Blue Well' or 'Well of Youth' is now known locally as the Wishing Well. Rising within a circular stone pool inside a walled enclosure, the chalybeate water overflows into a channel and stream stained orange. Coins lie in the small well chamber and clouties and carvings adorn nearby beeches. At one time the well had a female guardian. Before the war, coaches took crowds to visit on May Day, when coins were offered, wishes made and rags tied on nearby trees. The coins were later retrieved for local charities. A path leads westwards from the well to a silted-up stone-lined pool.

the Celtic year – were the most popular. Ritual at the well (also named after St Boniface, a local bishop) has become the usual pagan and Christian mix, with many variations: turn three times sunwise, spill the water three times from cupped hands, take three sips in the name of Father, Son and Holy Spirit, then tie an offering before making a wish. Some people collect the water in bottles and jerry cans; others just point video cameras out of car windows and drive away.

Charlton-on-Otmoor, Islip, Oxfordshire

A curfew used to be rung from the tower of St Mary the Virgin's Church every night between 18 October and 15 March to guide those lost in the wilderness of Ot Moor. An arrangement of box branches on a wooden frame adorns the sixteenth-century rood screen. Known as the 'May Cross', 'My Lady' or 'Our Lady', and always referred to as female, this anthropomorphic cross is taken down and dressed with fresh box and flowers for every May Day and village feast day, 19 September. Statues of St John and the Virgin flanking a central cross, broken up at the Reformation, were replaced by large hooped garlands of flowers surmounted with crosses. Two garlands are shown in an engraving of 1823; an illustration of 1840 has only one. A disapproving vicar had the garland taken away, but on his departure in 1854 the villagers replaced 'Our Lady of the Otmoor Towns'. Until 1857 two men carried the garland on a stick, followed by six morris dancers, a clown with bladder and money-box, and a man playing a pipe, with most of the village in procession behind.

Another account describes four strong young women carrying the figure across Ot Moor to be blessed by the prioress at Horton-cum-Studley. This was followed by dancing in the evening, when the cross was hoisted up on to the rood screen. The garland seems to have been a response to the destruction of 'popish' images, but her attributes are a subtle mixture of the Virgin Mary and Flora, the Italian goddess of spring and blossoming plants, whose festival was celebrated in the Roman world between 28 April and 3 May. The Ot Moor Lady is a reminder that images of a goddess were once carried around sacred precincts, and taken into the fields to bless and encourage the growing crops.

Tissington Well Dressings, Ashbourne, Derbyshire

Derbyshire is in the heart of England, but is an ancient place known for retaining its Celtic customs and folklore. In their present form, the famous well dressings are relatively recent – some were only begun or 'revived' this century – but there is general agreement that they hark back to pre-Christian customs. The Ascension Day dressings held at Tissington, whose waters are remarkably pure and unfailing, are probably the oldest, tracing their origins to celebrations after the terrible drought of 1615 or thanksgivings in 1350 by the villagers, who believed the water had helped them survive the Black Death. On Holy Thursday, after a church service, the priest and choir lead a procession around the wells, where a hymn or psalm is sung at each, a prayer offered and the water blessed. The adornment of the wells has become a skilful and highly organized undertaking. Biblical stories and scenes of contemporary and local interest are pressed on to large panels of clay, salted to keep it moist, using moss, flower petals, leaves, berries, pine cones, rice, haricot beans, linseed, coal, oatmeal and any other organic material imagination can find a use for. Gradually modern materials such as tin foil are being incorporated into the designs. Dressing are held throughout northern Derbyshire, mainly on Christian festivals and Bank Holidays, from the second half of May into September. Other counties such as Gloucestershire and Staffordshire hold them too. An annual outing from my junior school took us to Tissington on Ascension Day to walk the circular road around the village looking at the five decorated wells. This was followed by a visit to Dove Dale, where high spirits were let off by climbing the bare dome of

Thorpe Cloud before running down again over the grazed limestone pasture, whooping and shrieking out of exhilaration and fear. For a child of the Derby suburbs, the startlingly clean, stone-tasting water, the freshness of air and nearness of sky on exposed heights, and the wild, ancient strangeness of the Derbyshire countryside awakened longings – as strong as they were unrealistic – for a world I felt I had missed. Those trips to the wells began to give me a sense of older ways and intuitions underlying Christian tradition, and contributed to the jumble of ideas and feelings which helps me to recognize and define what is, for me, a holy place.

GAZETTEER OF SITES

HIS IS NOT A GUIDEBOOK, but I hope the following information and comments on the sites photographed will be of some interest and help in planning visits. The name and location are given, along with the Ordnance Survey 1:50,000 map sheet and National Grid reference; many of the sites are extremely difficult to find using only a motoring atlas or general tourist map. The owner or organization responsible for the site is listed, followed by comments on the remains and access, etc.

Cadw Welsh Historic Monuments, English Heritage, Historic Scotland and the National Trust all have membership schemes, publications, events and displays to help visitors appreciate and enjoy the properties and landscapes in their care.

The Council for British Archaeology, based in York (01904 671384), also has a national and local membership scheme (and the Young Archaeologists Club), designed to inform and involve those interested in all aspects of archaeology.

Alderley Edge Wells
Macclesfield, Cheshire, England
OS 118 (SJ 858779 and SJ 855781).
National Trust
Car park and information beside the Wizard on B5087 SE of Alderley Edge. Sandstone escarpment with mining from Bronze Age up to nineteenth century.

Bardsey Island (Ynys Enlli)
off Aberdaron, Lleyn, Gwynedd, Wales
OS 123 (SH 120222).
Bardsey Island Trust, tel: (01766) 514774
Visits to the island must be arranged in advance through the Trust. Good views from Braich y Pwll and Mynydd Mawr SW of Aberdaron. (*See also* St Mary's Well)

Bar Hill Roman Fort
Twechar, Strathclyde, Scotland
OS 64 (NS 707759).   Historic Scotland
Earthworks of fort and Antonine Wall; foundations of bathhouse and headquarters building with well. Information panels. Access by track running E from Twechar.

Bartlow Hills Burial Mounds
Linton, Cambridgeshire, England
OS 154 (TL 587448).
Cambridgeshire County Council
By Essex border between Ashdon and Linton. Footpath leads E from minor road S of Bartlow to three tumuli; the fourth is on private land N of the former railway line.

Bath, Roman Baths Museum
Pump Room, Abbey Churchyard, Somerset, England
OS 172 (ST 751647).
Bath City Council, tel: (01225) 477791
Breathtaking museum; display of baths and other Roman remains 20 feet below the Georgian town. The Pump Room dispenses refreshment and soothing doses of culture. Open daily, times vary. A spring also rises in the Cross Bath (ST 749646) in Hot Bath Street, SW of the museum.

Benwell Roman Temple
Newcastle upon Tyne, Tyne and Wear, England
OS 88 (NZ 217646).
English Heritage
Beside Broomridge Avenue in housing estate S of A186 Hexham road, SW outskirts of Newcastle. Replica altars. The vallum crossing is nearby (NZ 215646).

Boleigh Fogou
Lamorna, Penzance, Cornwall, England
OS 203 (NG 437252)
Centre for Alternative Education and Research
Underground passage and remains of a defended settlement. In the garden of Rosemerryn House, off B3315, in St Buryan parish. Standing stones, etc. nearby.

Bradwell-on-Sea, St Peter's Chapel

Maldon, Essex, England
OS 168 (TM 031082)
Drive along, then walk, the Roman road NE
of Bradwell. The chapel and Roman fort are
situated by the marshy shore with the
Othona Community to the N.

Brean Down Temple Site

Weston Bay, Somerset, England
OS 182 (ST 293588).   National Trust
Park at end of coast road N of Brean, steep
climb up cliff steps. No temple remains, but
important natural history site and relic
ancient landscape with a 'lost world' feel.

Burgh Castle Roman Fort and Monastic Site

Great Yarmouth, Norfolk, England
OS 134 (TG 475046).
English Heritage and Norfolk Archaeological
Trust
Access via minor roads off A143 SW of
Yarmouth. Fort overlooks eastern end of the
Breydon Water and Berney Arms Mill – good
waterside walks and views.

Burghead Promontory Fort and Well

Moray, Grampian, Scotland
OS 28 (NJ 109691).
Historic Scotland (Bailey's Well)
At the end of B9013 off A96(T) NW of Elgin.
Earthworks of upper and lower wards of the
fort are at the NW tip of the promontory; the
well is at the end of King Street.

Burry Holms Fort and Hermitage

The Gower, West Glamorgan, Wales
OS 159 (SS 401926)
Tidal island at the N end of Rhossili Bay, at
the western end of the Gower. Access via
footpaths through the Burrows (dunes) NW
of Llangennith.

Cadbury Castle Hillfort

South Cadbury, Somerset, England
OS 183 (ST 628252)
One of the best hillforts in England; famous
for late 1960s excavations and as a possible
location for King Arthur's Camelot. First
occupied in the Neolithic, refortified in the
fifth century AD, it contained an 'Arthurian-
period' feasting hall. Car park off minor road
just S of the village. Footpath to NE entrance
from S of church.

Caerwent Romano-Celtic Temple and Town

Chepstow, Gwent, Wales
OS 171 (ST 469905)   Cadw
Town walls; foundations of excavated
features, including houses and temple.
Roman inscriptions in church. Village s of
A48(T) Chepstow–Caerleon road.

Cairnpapple Hill Circle-Henge

Torpichen, West Lothian, Scotland
OS 65 (NS 987717).
Historic Scotland
Wide views from hilltop ceremonial site in
use from the Neolithic to the Iron Age. Site
display, information boards, reconstructed
Bronze Age grave inside mound.

Caldey Island Monastery and Priory

off Tenby, Dyfed, Wales
OS 158 (SS 141963 priory),
Reformed Cistercian Order
Boat trips from Tenby harbour, weekdays
early May to late September. Guided tours of
monastery for men only; other facilities and
monuments open to all.

Carn Ingli 'Mount of Angels'

Newport, Dyfed, Wales
OS 145 (SN 063372)
Footpaths lead to Mynydd Carningli s from
Newport and across Carningli Common.
Nevern church is at SN 083400, the pilgrim
cross at SN 081400.

Castell Henllys Fort

Felindre-Farchog, Newport, Dyfed, Wales
OS 145 (SN 117390).
Dyfed County Council
Settlement (c. 1000 BC–AD 60) defended
by earthworks and natural slopes.
Reconstructions based on excavation
details. Displays, ancient farm breeds.

Casterley Camp Hillfort and Sanctuary

Upavon, Wiltshire, England
OS 184 (SU 115535)
On the edge of an army artillery and tank
area. Approach cautiously by a minor road
SW of Upavon.

Castle Loch Sacred Lake

Lochmaben, Annadale and Eskdale,
Dumfries and Galloway, Scotland
OS 85 (NY 087815)

Sacred to the god Maponus. Renowned for its fish, including the rare and reclusive vendace, which appreciates the deep, clean, nutrient-poor waters.

Cerne Abbas, St Augustine's Well

Dorchester, Dorset, England
OS 194 (ST 666014)
In cemetery of the ruined abbey beside Abbey Farm, N of the church. Reached by a tree-lined sunken lane leading down below the level of the burial ground. The water flows out into the rear of the village pond, which fronts on to Abbey Street.

Cerne Giant Hill Figure

Cerne Abbas, Dorchester, Dorset, England
OS 194 (ST 666016).   National Trust
Viewing point, information boards in A352 lay-by NW of the village. The hilly B-road W of Cerne Abbas gives views of the giant and enclosure in their landscape.

Chalice Well Gardens

Glastonbury, Somerset, England
OS 182 & 183 (ST 052872).
Chalice Well Trust, tel: (01458) 831154
Beautiful, symbolic gardens around the Chalice Well head, stream and pilgrim bath. Open every day 10 a.m.–6 p.m. March–end October, 1 p.m.–4 p.m. November–end February. Access and small car park via Chilkwell Street (A361), SE of town centre.

Chanctonbury Ring Temple Site

Washington, West Sussex, England
OS 198 (TQ 139121)
Parking on trackway off E carriageway of A24 Worthing road, S of Washington. Walk South Downs Way to hillfort on edge of scarp. No access to interior, replanted after hurricane damage to trees. Dew pond to left of track approaching fort from W.

Charlton-on-Otmoor Church

Islip, Oxfordshire, England
OS 164 (SP 561158)
On Ot Moor E of A34 Oxford–Bicester road. The box-branch cross on the rood screen is dressed with flowers every May Day and 19 September.

Chester, Minerva Shrine

Edgar's Field, Cheshire, England
OS 117 (SJ 407656)

In a park S of the River Dee, immediately SW of Old Dee Bridge, not the A483(T).

Chittlehampton, St Hieritha's Church

South Molton, Devon, England
OS 180 (SS 636256)
Imposing late-Perpendicular church, paid for largely by offerings to St Urith's shrine, in village E of the River Taw and A377 Crediton–Barnstaple road.

Clackmannan Stone

Clackmannan, Stirling, Central, Scotland
OS 58 (NS 911918)
Boulder on monolith by Mercat Cross and Tolbooth tower in town centre. Reputed original site at NS 912911, W of road leading S from town towards River Forth.

Clochmaben Stone Celtic Sacred Site

Gretna, Annadale and Eskdale, Dumfries and Galloway, Scotland
OS 85 (NY 312660)
Two granite boulders, hidden in the fields W of minor road running to the shore from Old Graitney, SW of Gretna.

Coventina's Well

Carrawburgh, Hadrian's Wall, Northumberland, England
OS 87 (NY 857711)
On private land NW of the Temple of Mithras, 100 yards W of Brocolitia Roman fort – a marshy area bounded by a dry-stone wall and fencing.

Craigie Well

Avoch, Black Isle, Inverness, Highland, Scotland
OS 26 (NH 679532).
On a wooded hillside above N shore of Munlochy Bay, immediately E of sandstone quarry inlet. Private land, difficult access, hard to find. Visit the splendid Groam House Museum, Rosemarkie, to learn about the Picts.

Croft Ambrey Hillfort

Leominster, Hereford and Worcester, England
OS 137 (SO 444668) National Trust
Access from NW via track and footpath NE of Yatton, E of A4110, or from S in grounds of Croft Castle. Impressive ramparts, sanctuary site overgrown.

Danebury Ring Hillfort

Stockbridge, Hampshire, England
OS 185 (SU 323377)
Hampshire County Council
Country park: information boards, etc. with details from recent excavations directed by Professor Barry Cunliffe. Three lines of massive ramparts, complex E entrance.

Derwentwater Lake and St Herbert's Isle

Keswick, Cumbria, England
OS 90 (NY 259212).   National Trust
Good views and popular walks around lake. Hire boat from Keswick jetties or gaze down from Surprise View (NY 269195). Hordes of photographers at dawn and sunset, particularly by the jetties. Don't go in the school holidays.

Dinas Emrys Fort

Beddgelert, Gwynedd, Wales
OS 115 (SH 606492).
National Trust
Wooded rocky hill on N side of A498, NE of Beddgelert, SW of Llyn Dinas. Waymarked but difficult access via NE ridge. The whole site is both vulnerable and dangerous. Contact NT warden on (01766) 890293.

Dowloch (Black Loch)

Penpont, Dumfries and Galloway, Scotland
OS 78 (NX 839975)
At NE tip of Dhu Loch plantation, SW of Auchenknight farm on minor road N of Penpont, W of Thornhill on A702. Drumlanrig Castle is to NE, off A76.

Druid's Temple

Ilton, North Yorkshire, England
OS 99 (SE 175787)
Regency megalithic folly in Druid's Plantation, NW of Ilton and SW of Masham.

Dunadd Fort

Kilmartin Valley, Argyll, Scotland
OS 55 (NR 836935)
Historic Scotland
Signposted track W of A816, between Kilmartin and Lochgilphead. Parking and information. Defences on different levels. Rock basin below summit, with footprint, Ogham inscription and boar carving under a modern cast.

Dunino Den Pictish Ceremonial Site and Cross

St Andrews, Fife, Scotland
OS 59 (NO 540109)
Take minor road E of A959 at Dunino, SW of St Andrews, for Dunino Church. Follow footpath W, beyond graveyard into woods.

Eildon Hill North Fort

Melrose, Borders, Scotland
OS 73 (NT 555328)
Park in lay-by on N side of A6091, SE of Melrose, opposite footpath leading S to hillfort. Stiff climb is rewarded by good views.

Eileach an Naoimh Celtic Monastery

Garvellach Isles, Firth of Lorne, Argyll, Scotland
OS 55 (NM 640097).   Historic Scotland
Early Christian and medieval monastic remains on remote island associated with St Columba. If you don't own a yacht, try Peter and Christine Proudlove of Kingfisher Cruises, operating from Ardfern, on Loch Craignish, tel: (01852) 50662.

Farley Heath Temple Site

Albury, Guildford, Surrey, England
OS 187 (TQ 05174490).
The Hurtwood Control
On wooded heathland (privately owned common land) immediately W of minor road between Farley Green and Shamley Green, 2 miles S of Albury. The shallow depression of Skemp Pond is 100 yards SE at TQ 053448.

Ffynnon Gwenlais

Llandybie, Dyfed, Wales
OS 159 (SN 600161)
Well and yew visible from footpath to Carreg Gwenlais Farm, S of minor road between Pant-y-llyn and A476 below Carmel. The turlough 'winter lake' is at SN 606166, beside road S of Pant-y-llyn.

Flag Fen Archaeology Park

Fourth Drove, Fengate, Peterborough, Cambridgeshire England
OS 142 (TL 227989) Tel: (01733) 313414
Open daily 11 a.m.–4 p.m. (in summer 5 p.m.) except 25 and 26 December. Visitor centre, museum; preserved Bronze Age timbers; section through Roman road; re-creations of prehistoric buildings,

landscapes and technology; ancient species of farm animals; excavations (not winter). Wheelchair access and facilities, teachers' packs, videos.

Glastonbury Tor and St Michael's Tower

Somerset, England
OS 182 (ST 513386)   National Trust
Footpaths and very limited parking on Stone Down Lane and bottom of Wellhouse Lane, N of the A361. Look out for didgeridoos at dawn and sunset.

Gosbecks Archaeological Park

Colchester, Essex, England
OS 168 (TL 969226).
Colchester Archaeological Trust
Exhibition, information boards; ground plans of temple and theatre marked out in white – building a full-scale replica of the temple is planned. Access from Oliver's Lane,s from the road linking B1022 and B1026, 2 miles SW of Colchester centre.

Harlow Temple

Riverway, Temple Fields, Harlow, Essex, England
OS 167 (TL 468123)
Romano-Celtic temple marked out in modern materials in factory estate s of River Stort, w of Harlow Mill Station.

Hayling Island Temple Site

Havant, Hampshire, England
OS 197 (SU 724030)
No access to site, which is usually under a crop. Fully excavated, no visible remains. Field may be viewed from footpath between A3023 at Stoke and North Hayling Church. Cogidumnus's palace at Fishbourne (SU 841047) is open to the public.

Holy Island

Lamlash Bay, Arran, Scotland
OS 69 (NS 059296).
Samyê-Ling Tibetan Buddhists
Cave hermitage of St Molaise on rugged and beautiful island used as retreat by Tibetan Buddhists. Boat trips from Lamlash; no tourist facilities on the isle.

Holy Island (Lindisfarne)

Berwick upon Tweed, Northumberland, England
OS 75 (NU 126418).
English Heritage (priory and museum), National Trust (castle)
Causeway from Beal Sands E of A1 (T) between Alnwick and Berwick. Inaccessible two hours before and three hours after high tide – timetable at end of causeway.

Holywell, St Winefride's Chapel and Well

Clwyd, Wales
OS 116 (SY 183763).
Cadw and Delyn District Council
The well, and its former owner Basingwerk Abbey, are between the A55 and A548, along the Dee estuary, NW of Flint.

Ingleborough Hill and Fort

Ingleton, North Yorkshire, England
OS 98 (SD 741745)
Yorkshire Dales National Park
Millstone-grit walls enclose remains of round houses on summit plateau of 15 acres. Footpaths approach from N (Chapel le Dale on the Roman road, B6255) and from Ingleton to SW. Good views of hill from Twisleton Scars area to NW.

Iona Island

off the Ross of Mull, Argyll, Scotland
OS 48 (NM 287245).
Iona Cathedral Trust and National Trust for Scotland
Passenger ferry from Fionnphort on Mull. Most people visit Iona on ugly coach trips from Oban, rushing to the abbey in a blind frenzy.

Ippollits, St Hippolytus's Church

Hitchin, Hertfordshire, England
OS 166 (TL 198271)
Opposite school on minor roads between A602 and B656, SE of Hitchin, NW of Stevenage. Doors locked, no information about key.

Isle Maree

Loch Maree, Gairloch, Wester Ross, Highland, Scotland
OS 19 (NG 930723)
Visible from elevated roadside viewpoints at either end of loch. Inquire about hiring a boat and gillie from Loch Maree Hotel, beside A832, on widest part of loch.

Jordan Hill Temple

Weymouth, Dorset, England
OS 194 (SY 698821).   English Heritage
Stone foundations of central shrine of
Romano-Celtic temple. Good views of
Weymouth Bay. Access from Furzy Cliff road,
off A353, 2 miles NE of Weymouth.

Julian's Bower Turf Maze

Alkborough, Lincolnshire, England
OS 106 & 112 (SE 881217)
Interesting, remote corner; S of the Humber,
E of the Trent and N of Scunthorpe. Maze
pattern has been copied in floor of church
porch.

Lady's Well

Holystone, Rothbury, Northumberland,
England
OS 81 (NT 953029).   National Trust
Access via footpath from forestry car park,
beside road leading W from village.

Lindow Common Nature Reserve

Wilmslow, Cheshire, England
OS 109 (SJ 833812).
Macclesfield Borough Council
Lindow Man found in peat at SJ 820805, but
a better idea of the Iron Age landscape of
his death is obtained by walking among the
mire pools and birches of the reserve.

Llaneilian, St Eilian's Church and Chapel

Amlwch, Anglesey, Gwynedd, Wales
OS 114 (SH 469928)
Church is W of Amlwch, near Point Lynas. A
footpath leads N to Porth yr Ychen, then NW
along coast to ruined well chapel by a
stream at SH 46569329.

Llantwit Major, St Illtud's Church

Cowbridge, South Glamorgan, Wales
OS 170 (SS 966687)
Llanilltud Fawr, near the coast S of
Cowbridge, W of Cardiff, is a thriving church
with one of the longest histories of
continuous Christian worship in Britain.

Llyn Cerrig Bach Sacred Lake

Valley, Anglesey, Gwynedd, Wales
OS 114 (SH 306765)
Landscape of outcrops and small lakes N of
RAF Valley. Plaque, on large boulder at park-
ing place across road from N entrance of
airfield, commemorates the site.

Lullingstone Roman Villa

Eynsford, Sevenoaks, Kent, England
OS 177 (TQ 529651).   English Heritage
Access via A225 SW of Eynsford: take
junction 3 off M25 and follow A20 towards
Brands Hatch – good luck. Tel: (01322)
863467 for opening times.

Madron Well and Chapel

Penzance, Cornwall, England
OS 203 (SW 445328)
Madron is just NW of Penzance on B3312.
Track and footpath NW of village.

Maiden Castle Hillfort

Dorchester, Dorset, England
OS 194 (SY 672884).   English Heritage
Magnificent ramparts, remains of Romano-
Celtic temple in E enclosure. Access and
parking via minor road (off B3147), running
SW from Dorchester.

Maryport Roman Fort

Workington, Cumbria, England
OS 89 (NY 039373).
Museum tel: (01900) 816168
On the Sea Brows above N end of town.
Park at the Battery, home of superb
Senhouse Roman Museum, which is open
all year although days and times vary.
No access to fort.

Meavy Oak

Tavistock, Devon, England
OS 201 (SX 540672)
On green beside church in Meavy, E of
Yelverton. There is another fine oak (and a
stone cross just uphill from river) by ford SE
of village.

Mizmaze Turf Maze

Breamore Down, Hampshire, England
OS 184 (SU 141202)
Look at Breamore Saxon church, W of A338,
N of Fordingbridge. Follow footpath NW,
through Breamore House Wood, on to the
Down: maze signed to left.

Munlochy Well

Black Isle, Inverness, Scotland
OS 26 (NH 640537)
Beside lay-by on S side of A832, just NW of
Munlochy – not easy to miss. Look for
original spring which is uphill from modern
spout.

Nettleton Shrub (Scrubb) Temple Site

Castle Combe, Wiltshire, England
OS 173 (ST 822769)
Healing sanctuary site, now featureless
pasture W of Fosse Way, where it crosses
Broadmead Brook, 2 miles SW of M4.

Newstead Roman Fort (Trimontium)

Melrose, Borders, Scotland
OS 73 & 74 (NT 571346)
Memorial and slight remains either side of
dangerous B6361, S of the Tweed, W of
A68(T) crossing. Fort museum in Melrose
to W.

Newtondale Spring Healing Well

Cropton Forest, Pickering, North Yorkshire,
England
OS 100 (SE 841953).
Forest Enterprise
At base of rock face 300 feet W of Needle
Point. Access to platform built over cistern
is from a made pathway branching W from
footpath, downhill from Needle Point.

Norfolk Lavender Ltd

Caley Mill, Heacham, Norfolk, England
OS 132 (TF 685374).
Tel: (01485) 570384
This is not the site of the Snettisham
Treasure. Shop, visitors' centre, gardens,
tea-room open all year. Tours of lavender
fields – harvesting around mid-July to mid-
August.

Overton, St Mary's Church

Wrexham, Clwyd, Wales
OS 117 (SJ 373418)
A pre-Christian yew stands in NW corner of
churchyard. Collection of over 20 yews
considered to be among the 'Seven Wonders
of Wales'.

Partrishow (Patricio), St Issui's Church and Well

Abergavenny, Powys, Wales
OS 161 (SO 279224 & SO 278223)
Partrishow is defended by steep, narrow,
difficult lanes, approached by turning W off
B4423 Llanthony road at Stanton. Park by
well; space for two cars at lychgate.

Pennant Melangell Church and Shrine

Llangynog, Powys, Wales
OS 125 (SJ 02352655)

Tucked away in Cwm Pennant, W of
Llangynog on A4391 Bala–Oswestry road.
The valley road is single-track and there are
no facilities for tourists.

Pistyll, St Beuno's Church

Nefyn, Lleyn, Gwynedd, Wales
OS 123 (SH 328423)
On pilgrim route to Bardsey, ancient Celtic
church decorated at Christmas, Easter and
Lammas. Turn N off B4417 between Llithfaen
and Nefyn.

Puffin Island and Penmon Priory

Anglesey, Gwynedd, Wales
OS 115 (SH 630806).
Cadw (priory and dovecote)
Penmon priory is NE of Beaumaris. No
access to Puffin Island: good views from
Penmon Point and coast road between
Bangor and Llandudno.

River Witham

Tattershall Bridge, Lincolnshire, England
OS 122 (TF 197562)
Ferry replaced by bridge, superseded by new
A153; old bridge remains beside upgraded
section. Bronze boar's head dredged from
ferry crossing in 1768; two bronze swords
found to N at the confluence with Billinghay
Skirth.

Roche Rock Chapel, Cross and Holy Well

Roche, St Austell, Cornwall, England
OS 200 (SW 991596)
St Michael's is beside road, SE of B3274 at St
Gonan's Church and cross (SW 988598). Well
(SW 984618) on private property is accessible
by footpath N of A30.

Runnymede Bridge and River Thames

Egham, Surrey, England
OS 176 (TQ 019719)
Bronze Age settlement site and old river
course buried beneath S approach ramps.
Possible to walk along S side of Thames and
under bridges.

St Anne's Well

Buxton, Derbyshire, England
OS 119 (SK 057735)
Spa and market town high in the Peak
District with beautiful gardens. Crescent and
Pavilion. St Anne's, and another well in
Market Place nearby, dressed mid-July.

St Blane's Monastery

Kingarth, Isle of Bute, Strathclyde, Scotland
OS 63 (NS 095534).
Historic Scotland.
Signposted on minor road to Dunagoil from A844, just SW of Kingarth.

St Clether Chapel and Holy Well

Launceston, Cornwall, England
OS 201 (SX 203846)
Village of St Clether is S of A395, Launceston–Bude road. A footpath from S of church runs NW to chapel above N bank of River Inny.

St Columba's Cave,

Loch Caolisport, Knapdale, Argyll, Scotland
OS 62 (NR 751768)
On N shore near head of loch between Cove and Ellary. Turn off B8024 at Achahoish, SW of Lochgilphead. No through road to Kilmory and Loch Sween.

St Columba's Footsteps

Keil Point, Southend, Kintyre, Scotland
OS 68 (NR 673077)
Carved footprints on knoll W of Columba's chapel. In cliff to W is Keil Cave; holy well to E behind graveyard. Parking and information.

St David's Cathedral

St David's, Dyfed, Wales
OS 157 (SM 751254).
Cadw (Bishop's Palace)
Small city at end of Pembrokeshire's NW peninsula. Church, palace and other buildings stand within a cathedral close, defended by a wall and gatehouses.

St Fillan's Pool and Priory

Strath Fillan, Stirling, Central, Scotland
OS 50 (NN 351288 & NN 359285)
On West Highland Way NE of A82(T) between Crianlarich and Tyndrum. Priory ruins and information at Kirkton Farm; the pool is opposite St Fillan's Church.

St Finnan's Isle

Loch Shiel, Lochaber, Highland, Scotland
OS 40 (NM 752683)
Turn off west coast road (A861) for Dalelia, between Langal and Ardmolich. Walk E from pier for glimpse of island; it may be possible to hire boat at Dalelia farmhouse.

St Gwenfaen's Well

Rhoscolyn, Anglesey, Wales
OS 114 (SH 259754)
Rhoscolyn is reached by minor roads off B4545 SW of Valley. Well is on coastal footpath, accessible from Borthwen or lane and footpath NW of church.

St Mary's Well

Culloden, Inverness, Scotland
OS 27 (NH 723453)
Beside footpath in a wood; access via Blackpark Farm from B9006, off A9 SE of Inverness. Also visit Clava chambered cairns and Culloden battlefield.

St Mary's Well (Ffynnon Fair)

Aberdaron, Lleyn, Gwynedd, Wales
OS 123 (SH 13922518).
National Trust
NT car park at bottom of Mynydd Mawr, SW of Aberdaron. Rock steps lead right from beside stream as it enters tiny inlet. Not accessible at high tide; dangerous and difficult to find. Coins in spring crevice.

St Melor's Well

Linkinhorne, Cornwall, England
OS 201 (SX 318732)
Fifteenth-century well house with statue niche above door and internal shelf. Above small stream at bottom of private fields SW of Linkinhorne church.

St Nectan's Kieve

Tintagel, Cornwall, England
OS 200 (SX 081885)
Waterfall and rock basin in secluded valley E of Tintagel. Access by lane from Trethevey. Hermitage Tea Gardens are on site of Nectan's cell.

St Ninian's Cave

Physgill, Whithorn, Wigtown, Dumfries and Galloway, Scotland
OS 83 (NX 422359).
Historic Scotland.
Walk through bluebell woods of Physgill Glen, SW of Whithorn, to Port Castle Bay; cave is along beach to right.

St Ninian's Isle Chapel

Bigton, South Mainland, Shetland, Scotland
OS 4 (HU 368208)
Access via A970 and B9122 S of Lerwick.

Track from Bigton to car park; walk across sand spit, which is very occasionally cut off by tide.

St Non's Well
Altarnun, Cornwall, England
OS 201 (SX 224815)
Well and bowssening pool; on private land NE of church and Celtic cross.

St Non's Well and Chapel
St David's, Dyfed, Wales
OS 157 (SM 751243).
Cadw (chapel)
Lane due S of St Davids leads to St Non's Retreat spiritual centre. Modern 'Celtic' chapel by house. Well and ruined chapel downhill from car park.

Sancreed Holy Well
West Penwith, Cornwall, England
OS 203 (SW 41782930)
Footpath runs SW from Sancreed churchyard. 'Healing Springs of St Euny' (SW 39972890), and Carn Euny courtyard houses and fogou (SW 40242885) nearby.

Schiehallion Sacred Mountain
Kinloch Rannoch, Perth and Kinross, Tayside, Scotland
OS 52 (NN 713547)
Good views of mountain from shore of Loch Rannoch.

Sherwood Forest Country Park
Edwinstowe, Nottinghamshire, England
OS 120 (SK 623678).
Nottinghamshire County Council
Some 450 acres of ancient forest famous for Major Oak (SK 621679) and Robin Hood. Visitor's centre, trails, information panels. Wheelchair access and facilities.

Steep Holme Island
Bristol Channel, Somerset, England
OS 182 (ST 229607)
Good views from Brean Down and Weston-super-Mare.

Swastika Stone Rock Carving
Ilkley, West Yorkshire, England
OS 104 (SE 09554696)
In railings on Addingham High Moor, SW of Ilkley. Roads wind up out of town, with footpaths on to moors past reservoir. Around

parish church, N of A65 in centre of town, are carved crosses, rock carvings, wall of Roman fort and Manor House Museum.

Syon Reach, River Thames
Brentford, Middlesex, England
OS 176 (TQ 174764)
Pleasant riverside walk between Richmond and Kew – but danger of impact with cyclists, joggers, push-chairs.

Tarren Deusant Pagan Cult Site
Beddau, Llantrisant, Mid-Glamorgan, Wales
OS 170 (ST 052872)
Rock face with 'Celtic head' carvings and a spring, on W side of Nantcastellau, SW of Pontypridd. In trees W of river and E of minor road running NE past Castellau and Lie'r Gaer. Accessible by footpaths, but on private land and difficult to find.

Temple of Mithras
Carrawburgh, Hadrian's Wall, Northumberland, England
OS 87 (NY 858711).   English Heritage
Car park and information beside B6318. Also Brocolitia fort and Coventina's Well.

Tigh nam Bodach
Glen Lyon, Perthshire, Tayside, Scotland
OS 51; 1:25,000 sheets 320 & 321 (NN 38044271)
A rough 6-mile walk from Lubreoch Dam. Glen Lyon is remarkable: call at Post Office, Shop and Tearoom (Bridge of Balgie) for supplies, refreshments and a chat.

Tissington Well Dressings
Ashbourne, Derbyshire, England
OS 119 (SK 176522)
E of A515, N of Ashbourne: annual decoration of five wells on Ascension Day.

Uffington White Horse
Wantage, Oxfordshire, England
OS 174 (SU 301866).
English Heritage and National Trust
Walk along Ridgeway path from Wayland's Smithy megalithic tomb (SU 281854, English Heritage) a mile to SW, or track runs S from B4507 to car park.

Virtuous Well
Trellech, Monmouth, Gwent, Wales
OS 162 (SO 503051)

Signed beside minor road SE of village, which is on B4293 S of Monmouth. Harold's Stones are beside B-road SW of village.

Well of the Heads
Loch Oich, Invergarry, Highland, Scotland
OS 34 (NN 304992)
Well and monument beside loch and A82(T), Spean Bridge–Fort Augustus road.

Wetwang Grange
Great Driffield, East Yorkshire, England
OS 101 & 106 Iron Age cemetery centred on SE 953600
Footpaths allow views of gravel workings and reconstituted farmland in valley used for settlement, burial and ritual. Access from A166 between Wetwang and Garton. In November 1995 the quarry had reached SE 938598, heading W to Station Farm.

Wilsford Shaft
Longbarrow Cross Roads, Amesbury, Wiltshire, England
OS 184 (SU 10864147)
Featureless field beside lay-by on terrifying A303(T). Normanton Down barrows to SE, impressive Winterbourne Stoke barrows to NW, Stonehenge a mile NE.

Wing Turf Maze
Uppingham, Leicestershire, England
OS 141 (SK 895028).
Wing is S of Oakham and Rutland Water. Maze is in wooden railings just S of village beside minor road leading to A47(T).

Wistman's Wood
Princetown, Dartmoor, Devon, England
OS 191 (SX 612773).
Duchy of Cornwall and English Nature
Two patches of oak woodland in valley of West Dart river, reached by footpath N from Two Bridges. Forest Nature Reserve with an ancient, mysterious atmosphere.

Woodeaton Temple Site
Islip, Oxfordshire, England
OS 164 (SP 537125)
Footpath cutting corner between Woodeaton road and B4027 to Islip gives access to bottom of hillside. Site in second field up; no visible remains.

Wookey Hole Caves
Wells, Somerset, England
OS 182 & 183 (ST 531480).
Tel: (01749) 672243
Open daily except week before Christmas. Allow two hours plus for guided tour of caves and other attractions, including paper mill and Victorian fairground. Objects in museum date back to Palaeolithic occupation of caves 50,000 years ago.

Wren's Egg Glacial Erratic and Standing Stones
Blairbuie, Monreith, Wigtown, Dumfries and Galloway, Scotland
OS 83 (NX 361419).   Historic Scotland
In a field W of Blairbuie farm track leading from minor road between A747 and A714 SE of Port William.

BIBLIOGRAPHY

I was greatly assisted by articles and reports in the following:

Antiquity, a quarterly journal published by Oxford University Press, edited by Christopher Chippindale

Britannia, a journal published by the Society for the Promotion of Roman Studies

British Archaeology, ten issues a year, published by the Council for British Archaeology, edited by Simon Denison

Current Archaeology, published six times a year by Andrew and Wendy Selkirk

I also used the *Royal Commission Inventories* and the *Victoria County Histories* for several counties and regions. My other main sources are listed below:

Adkins, L. and R. A *Thesaurus of British Archaeology*, David & Charles, Newton Abbot, 1982

Alcock, L. 'By South Cadbury is that Camelot . . .', Thames & Hudson, London, 1972

Allchin, A. *Pennant Melangell Place of Pilgrimage*, Gwasg Santes Melangell, 1994.

Anderson, W. and Hicks, C. *Holy Places of the British Isles*, Ebury Press, London, 1983

Ashe, G. *The Landscape of King Arthur*, Michael Joseph, London, 1978

Ashmore, B. *Senhouse Roman Museum*, Senhouse Museum Trust, Maryport, 1991

Barber, C. *Mysterious Wales*, Paladin, London. 1987
More Mysterious Wales, Paladin, London, 1987

Baring-Gould, S. and Fisher, J. *The Lives of the British Saints*, 4 vols., 1907–13

Bede, the Venerable, A *History of the English Church and People* (trans. L. Sherley-Price), Penguin Books, Harmondsworth, 1968

Bellhouse, R. *Joseph Robinson of Maryport*, Smith Settle, Otley, 1992

Berresford Ellis, P. A *Guide to Early Celtic Remains in Britain*, Constable, London, 1991

Brothwell, D. *The Bogman and the Archaeology of People*, British Museum, London, 1986

Burke, J. *Roman England*, Weidenfeld & Nicolson, London, 1983

Burl, A. *The Stone Circles of the British Isles*, Yale University Press, London, 1977
Rites of the Gods, Dent, London, 1981

Butler, A. (rev. H. Thurston and D. Attwater) *Lives of the Saints*, Burns & Oates, London, 1956

Caesar, J. *The Conquest of Gaul*, (trans. S. A. Handford), Penguin Books, Harmondsworth, 1978

Cavendish, R. *Prehistoric England*, Weidenfeld & Nicolson, London, 1983

Celts: Europe's People of Iron, Time–Life Books, Virginia, USA, 1994

Cunliffe, B. *Iron Age Communities in Britain*, Routledge & Kegan Paul, London, 1978.
Danebury, Anatomy of an Iron Age Hillfort, Batsford, London, 1983
The Roman Baths: A View over 2000 Years, BAT, Bath, 1993

Darvill, T. *Prehistoric Britain*, Batsford, London, 1987
Glovebox Guide: Ancient Britain, AA Publishing, Basingstoke, 1988

Dixon, J. *Gairloch and Guide to Loch Maree*, Nevisprint, Fort William, 1984 (reprint of the 1886 edition by Co-operative Printing Company, Edinburgh)

Dyer, J. *Ancient Britain*, Batsford, London, 1990

English Heritage Visitors' Handbook 1996–97, London, 1996

Evans, G. *The Pattern Under the Plough*, Faber & Faber, London, 1974
Ask the Fellows Who Cut the Hay, Faber & Faber, London, 1975

Farmer, D. *The Oxford Dictionary of Saints*, Oxford University Press, Oxford, 1979

Ferguson, J. An Illustrated Encyclopaedia of Mysticism and the Mystery Religions, Thames & Hudson, London, 1976

Godwin, M. The Holy Grail, Labyrinth/Bloomsbury, London, 1994

Goscinny and Uderzo, Asterix and the Cauldron, Hodder & Stoughton, London, 1978

Green, M. A Corpus of Religious Material from the Civilian Areas of Roman Britain, BAR no. 24, Oxford, 1976
The Gods of the Celts, Alan Sutton, Gloucester, 1986
The Sun-Gods of Ancient Europe, Batsford, London, 1991

Grimal, P. (ed.) Larousse World Mythology, Hamlyn, London, 1984

Guirand, F. (ed.) New Larousse Encyclopedia of Mythology, Hamlyn, London, 1984

Hall, J. Dictionary of Subjects and Symbols in Art, John Murray, London, 1989

Hawkes, J. A Guide to the Prehistoric and Roman Monuments in England and Wales, Chatto & Windus, London, 1976

Hedges, J. (ed.) The Carved Rocks on Rombolds Moor, West Yorkshire Metropolitan County Council,Wakefield, 1986

Henig, M. Religion in Roman Britain, Batsford, London, 1984

Hogg, A. Hill-Forts of Britain, Hart-Davis MacGibbon, London, 1975

Hole, C. English Folklore, Batsford, London, 1944–5

Houlder, C. Wales: An Archaeological Guide, Faber & Faber, London, 1978

John, C. The Saints of Cornwall, Dyllansow Truran, Redruth, 1981

Jones, F. The Holy Wells of Wales, University of Wales Press, Cardiff, 1992

Jones, G. and T. (trans.) The Mabinogion, Dent (Everyman), London, 1975

Kightly, C. and Cyprien, M. A Traveller's Guide to Places of Worship, Routledge & Kegan Paul, London, 1986

Lucan, Pharsalia (trans. R. Graves), Penguin Books, Harmondsworth, 1956

Lynch, F. Prehistoric Anglesey, Anglesey Antiquarian Society, Llangefni, 1991
A Guide to Ancient and Historic Wales: Gwynedd, HMSO, London, 1995

MacDonald, M. The Islands of Nether Lorne, West Highlands Publications, 1983

Mackie, E. Scotland: An Archaeological Guide, Faber & Faber, London, 1975

Megaw, J. and Simpson, D. Introduction to British Prehistory, Leicester University Press, Leicester, 1979

Merrifield, R. The Archaeology of Ritual and Magic, Batsford, London, 1987

Mildren, J. Saints of the South West, Bossiney Books, Bodmin, 1989

Millard, Dom B. (ed.) The Book of Saints, A & C Black, London, 1989

Morris, R. Churches in the Landscape, Dent, London, 1989

Muir, R. Riddles in the British Landscape, Thames & Hudson, London, 1981

National Trust, Properties of the National Trust, London, 1992
National Trust Countryside Handbook (compiled C. Spouncer), London, 1993
National Trust Handbook, London, 1996

Neal, D. Lullingstone Roman Villa, English Heritage, London, 1991

Piggott, S. Ancient Europe, Edinburgh University Press, Edinburgh, 1973
The Druids, Thames & Hudson, London, 1985

Pochin Mould, D. Scotland of the Saints, Batsford, London, 1952

Potter, B. The Tale of Squirrel Nutkin, Frederick Warne, London, 1903

Rackham, O. Trees and Woodland in the British Landscape, Dent, London, 1976
The Illustrated History of the Countryside, Weidenfeld & Nicolson, London, 1994

RCAHMS, Exploring Scotland's Heritage, 8 vols., HMSO, Edinburgh, 1985–87

RCHME, Stonehenge and Its Environs, Edinburgh University Press, Edinburgh, 1979

Renfrew, C. (ed.) British Prehistory: A New Outline, Duckworth, London, 1974

Ritchie, W. and G. Celtic Warriors, Shire, Princes Risborough, 1985

Roberts, T. Celtic Myths and Legends, Metro Books, USA, 1995

Robinson, B. and Gregory, T. Norfolk Origins 3: Celtic Fire and Roman Rule, Poppyland Publishing, North Walsham, 1987

Rodwell, W. (ed.) Temples, Churches and Religion in Roman Britain, BAR no. 77, Oxford, 1980

Ross, A. 'Shafts, Pits, Wells – Sanctuaries of the Belgic Britons?' in Coles, J. and Simpson, D. (eds.) *Studies in Ancient Europe*, Leicester University Press, Leicester, 1968
Everyday Life of the Pagan Celts, Carousel, London, 1972
Pagan Celtic Britain, Cardinal, London, 1974

Ross, A. *The Folklore of the Scottish Highlands*, Batsford, London, 1990

Ross, A. and Cyprien, M. *A Traveller's Guide to Celtic Britain*, Routledge & Kegan Paul, London, 1985

Ross, A. and Feacham, R. 'Ritual Rubbish? The Newstead Pits', in Megaw, J. (ed.) *To Illustrate the Monuments*, Thames & Hudson, London, 1976

Ross, A. and Robbins, D. *The Life and Death of a Druid Prince*, Rider, London, 1989

Russell, V. *West Penwith Survey*, Cornwall Archaeological Society, Truro, 1971

Salway, P. *The Oxford Illustrated History of Roman Britain*, Oxford University Press, Oxford, 1993

Scarre, C. (ed.) *Past Worlds, The Times Atlas of Archaeology*, Times Books, London, 1988
Timelines of the Ancient World, Dorling Kindersley, London, 1993

Sharkey, J. *Celtic Mysteries*, Thames & Hudson, London, 1975

Tacitus, C. *The Agricola and The Germania*, (trans. H. Mattingly, rev. S. A. Handford), Penguin Books, Harmondsworth, 1977

Thomas, C. *Celtic Britain*, Thames & Hudson, London, 1986

Tierney, J. 'The Celtic Ethnography of Posidonius', *Proceedings of the Royal Irish Academy* 60, 1960

Turner, R. and Scaife. *Bog Bodies*, British Museum, London, 1995

Underwood, G. *The Pattern of the Past*, Abacus, London, 1974

Wacher, J. *Roman Britain*, Dent, London, 1978

Wait, G. *Ritual and Religion in Iron Age Britain*, BAR British Series 149 (I) & (II), Oxford, 1985

Wedlake, W. *The Excavation of the Shrine of Apollo at Nettleton, Wiltshire 1956–1971*, Society of Antiquaries, London, 1982

Wilson, R. *A Guide to the Roman Remains in Britain*, Constable, London, 1988

Wood, E. *Collins Field Guide to Archaeology in Britain*, Collins, London, 1972

Woodward, A. *Shrines and Sacrifice*, Batsford/English Heritage, London, 1992

Wookey Hole Caves Ltd, *The Caves and Mill*, Cradley Holdings plc, 1995

INDEX OF SITES